MW00586546

Wealth Building AXIOMS Volume 1

Learn How You Can Use Financial Axioms to Stay Focused & Achieve More Throughout Your Lifetime...

Wealth Building Axioms Designed to
Encourage and Inspire You
Throughout Your Lifetime

THOMAS (TJ) UNDERWOO

Wealth Building AXIOMS Volume 1

Part of The Real Estate & Personal Finance 360 Degrees Series of Books

Thomas (TJ) Underwood

e-mail: tj@TheWealthIncreaser.com

Publisher: TFA Financial Planning

ISBN: 978-1-953994-18-9

Printed in the United States of America

©Thomas (TJ)) Underwood

Library of Congress Cataloging-in-Publication Data

Thomas (TJ) Underwood

Wealth Building AXIOMS Volume 1: A concise and to the point guide on how you can use empowering axioms to encourage and inspire you to achieve the goals that you desire most in a more efficient and effective manner at the various stages in your life.

Printed in the United States of America

Self-Published

Text design by Thomas (TJ) Underwood

Part of The Real Estate & Personal Finance 360 Degrees Series of Books

Acknowledgments

I owe much to my family, who have put up with me for several years during good and bad times during the creation of books in this series, and others from all walks of life who are a part of my life and are the source of inspiration for much of the material in this book.

A special thanks to my wife, Zelda for always believing in me.

Introduction

Over the years I have created many pages of content on several blogs, websites, and books.

In this compact book, select wealth building axioms or helpful thoughts that can be of great benefit to you and others, were assembled (360 in total) to help motivate you and others as you pursue improving your finances and making your dreams come true.

They are assembled in a sincere attempt to provide you added "mental insight and mental energy" as you pursue the goals that are most important to you.

Your building of wealth does not have to be a burdensome and boring process if you choose a more engaging and appropriate path toward the success that you truly desire.

In this helpful guide you will find axioms or wise sayings that have assisted many as they managed their finances and worked toward the building of wealth in a more lasting and permanent manner.

The following axioms came from inspiration that was received—and inspiration that was acted upon over several years.

The results of that inspiration and action that was acted upon are presented in this timely book so that you can get started towards the wealth building success that you desire and gain the knowledge that you need to know and apply appropriately that can lead to positive results that will show throughout your life—and even after you transition.

By comprehending the following axioms on a consistent schedule, you can position yourself for more success and gain added ammunition that can lead to you giving it your absolute best as you implement the management of your finances as you pursue wealth building success.

Wealth Building AXIOMS are part of a multi-year vision to present to you and others who desire lasting wealth building success added insight on how you can get there more efficiently. The goal is to create several volumes (with

360 Axioms per volume) from the year 2024 to the year 2036.

Below you will find the Volume 1 of 360 axioms that are provided to help you achieve at a higher level of excellence. Whether you read one axiom per day or multiple axioms per day, be sure to give serious thought to each axiom and how you can improve your life and wealth building future.

1)

Why let worry, fear and anxiety dominate your thoughts on a daily basis when you have the ability to change that and <u>dominate your thoughts </u>with <u>success</u>, <u>faith</u> and <u>certainty</u> as it relates to your credit and financial future—and life?

2)

You must realize that it is <u>your responsibility </u>to use your mind in a manner that benefits you and your family the most—not creditors and others who have no real concern for your or your family's future!

3)

You must realize that the adversity that you are now facing or that you may face in your future will make you stronger in the long run—if you believe it to be so! You must still visualize what you need to do as you must stay in the know.

4)

Did you know that when you know you can succeed you don't worry about failing or what others may think?

The true knowledge of how to attain the success that you desire can be found by looking within.

You can <u>choose to</u> over-use your mind, use your mind appropriately or under-use your mind. You decide how much success you can attain—or not!

5)

Did you know that if you change your thoughts and daily actions you can <u>change the direction</u> of your credit and financial future—right now?

It is important that you look for <u>and expect success on a daily basis!</u> Did you know that <u>daily griping and grumbling</u> will only lead to your stumbling?

6)

Now is the time that you start addressing the issues of concern in your life so that you can avoid financial strife.

Now is the time that you move forward—toward your reward and improve your scorecard!

7)

Always remember that success is not for you if you are not for success! When proper preparation, execution and the right knowledge meet up in your mind—success will say—WELCOME!

8)

By <u>acting immediately,</u> you can bring into reality that which you desire the most. Did you know that you have the <u>mental capacity</u> to do much more than you are currently doing in your life?

9)

Now is the time that you <u>use your mental energy and focus</u> to change your approach and get into the habit of taking **direct action** immediately on <u>matters that are of greatest concern</u> in your and your family's life!

10)

You must <u>get your mental energy up</u> and <u>pursue your goals and objectives</u> with the real expectation that they will occur!

You must meet that expectation head on by putting forth the <u>"required effort"</u> that is needed to bring into existence that which you desire most— now <u>at this present time!</u>

11)

If you <u>make the decision</u> to pursue what you desire at a higher level right now— you can bring into existence that which you desire most!

Why live your life <u>half-heartedly</u> when you have inside of you the ability to exert more effort and truly <u>reach the goals and objectives</u> that serves your and your family's best interest—not creditors?

12)

Even though <u>you may feel exhausted on a daily basis</u>—if you get started and believe in a <u>sincere way</u> that you will reach your <u>goals and objectives</u>, you can not only do so—you can also "increase" your <u>mental energy</u> to a higher level!

By taking **"direct action"** as it relates to your credit and finances <u>you will not procrastinate</u> and you will <u>move to action</u> in a consistent and highly effective manner.

13)

Now is the time that you take **"direct action"** and make your and your family's <u>dreams and goals a reality</u> at this particular time!

Now is the time that you <u>supercharge your mind</u> and work toward the success that you desire for yourself and your family!

14)

Emergency Funds are often difficult to establish for many due to inadequate income (all income is needed for daily living), lack of focus, lack of awareness and with many they just plainly don't want an **emergency fund** as they feel all their income outside of daily living should be invested in assets that provide a better return than that of a **money market account** or **CD.**

This can often be the wrong approach as the account could lose substantial value. However, many use this approach due to not properly understanding the "purpose" of an **emergency fund. Don't let that be you!**

15)

You must gain the <u>clear</u> <u>vision</u> that is needed for success **<u>throughout your lifetime</u>** and understanding your finances with clarity will help you <u>fine tune your</u>

focus and increase your commitment level so that you can attain the goals that you desire for yourself and your family.

16)

Debt pay-off or debt pay-down can occur, saving for that dream vacation can occur, saving for that second home can occur, that membership at LA Fitness can occur, funding your retirement account at the level that will ensure a pleasant retirement can occur—if you do what you need to do consistently!

17)

If you are one who currently lack the energy and strength that is needed to do what you need to do on a daily basis to maximize your future financial success, you must discover what you can do to change that.

There are many things that you can do to change that—and it is your responsibility to know what those things are and more importantly it is your responsibility to do those things so that you can achieve more!

18)

You must never be controlled by what has happened to you in your past—unless you are controlled in a manner that you benefit by what has happened in your past.

That means leaving past failures in the past, so they have no negative bearing on your present or future! That does not mean that you don't learn from your past (for example, you say to yourself—<u>I can't make that mistake again</u> and furthermore you must live for the present and future in a manner that shows you meant what you said)!

19)

You must **operate in integrity** and <u>you must be of the highest character.</u> In addition <u>you must let inspiration flow in</u> **and you must receive** and **act on** that inspiration when it is in your best interest to do so!
<u>By doing so you can increase your energy level significantly!</u>

You must act on the inspiration that is in your best interest in a <u>determined manner</u> and at the same time realize that there will always be risks whenever you are venturing into something new.

20)

You have more energy on the inside of you than you ever imagined.

Now is the time that you re-energize your mind and body and achieve the goals that serve your and your family's best interest!

You must determine what is causing your **fatigue** and you must learn from what is causing your **fatigue**—and **any other factor** that you feel is making your life more difficult.

21)

If you are **now ready to read**—you can obtain the knowledge that you need to succeed—and at the same time **reduce your fatigue!** You control what enters your mind and the management of your daily thoughts—use that control to reach higher and achieve more!

22)

Not knowing where you are headed and not understanding where you are at—is a leading cause of stress in the lives of those who do not have an effective plan—or system of credit and finance management in place.

Your goal is to know where you are headed and know where you are—by knowing that and more—you can go very far!

23)

You must realize that many let the **stress and uncertainty** of their credit and finances negatively affect their lifestyle. Many are on the verge of having a heart attack or stroke—or suffer a high level of stress in their daily life due to <u>frustration and uncertainty</u> over their credit and finances!

By not addressing their finances in a **timely** and **<u>appropriate manner</u>** they often carry the stress of the situation for months—and even years in some cases—inside of their mind and heart!

Don't let that be you, as you must know what you need to do to make your dreams come true!

24)

If you are currently in a position where your monthly income is insufficient to cover your monthly expenses you must address that by **coming up with a plan** to increase your income—cut your expenses—or doing a combination of the two.

If you are unable to do that and you find yourself in a situation where you can't pay off your revolving debt effectively over the next 4 to 5 years—you may need to consider <u>bankruptcy as a real option</u> prior to wiping out your retirement accounts and other accounts—not after!

25)

You must not do like many who go to attorney's and other professionals well after their credit and finances have bottomed out.

You must realize that you have <u>better options</u> that you can utilize if you are "proactive" and you address your concerns in a <u>timely manner.</u>

You must decide if you want to gain the **preparation** and **knowledge** that is needed for success in your future at this time—or do you want to gain the preparation and knowledge the "hard way" (after you make mishaps in the management of your credit and finances)!

26)

You no longer have to <u>make excuses or try to come up with reasons why you can't succeed</u> in your and your family's credit and financial future—or in any area of your life!

Now is the time that you move forward <u>and operate from a position of strength!</u> Now is the time that you reach higher so that you can achieve the success that you desire!

27)

Those who have **a financially alert mind** know how to <u>invest in a manner that serves their best long-term interests</u> and they <u>cannot be led astray by scammers and others</u> who do not have their best interest in mind.

Now is the time that you learn what you need to know so that you can achieve results that will show and put into action a financially alert mind so that you can truly grow.

28)

By gaining the knowledge that you need to succeed you put yourself in position to take your credit and financial success higher so that you can achieve the goals that you and your family desire.

By making a <u>real commitment</u> to use your mind in a **financially alert manner** you can put yourself in position to achieve your and your family's financial mission!

29)

By <u>opening your mind up to what is possible</u> you put yourself in control of your credit and finances and your future!

A **Financially Alert Mind** allows you to do your own thinking and allows **<u>you</u>** to

"take action" on your own initiative and empowers you with the ability to achieve the goals that serve your and your family's best interest.

You won't have to be forced or inspired by others to act—you will act on your own initiative to create the future that you desire!

30)

Did you know that if you have the self-discipline, proper preparation, proper focus and the right knowledge that is necessary you can manage many or all of the credit and financial affairs in your life?

Always realize that if you can control your thought process and direct your actions the right way—you can control your future!

31)

You can choose to "build up" your future or "tear down" your future by your daily thoughts and by the actions that you take on a consistent basis!

Did you know that a **F**inancially **A**lert **M**ind **I**mproves **L**ives **Y**early?

By having a **Financially Alert Mind** you can put yourself and your family in position to reach many or all of your future goals that you desire and you can position yourself to attain the goals that can make a real difference in your and your family's life!

You can now show your **LOVE** to your family and benefit your **F A M I L Y** and yourself by having a **Financially Alert Mind**—This Year!

32)

An experienced and highly competent money management personality will look at the external environment (political, regulatory, economic, social, technological and legal) as well as their goals, risk tolerance level, income and personal situation and analyze their personal financial statements and demographics to determine the best approach for meeting their financial **goals and objectives**.

You want to take steps to ensure that you have a highly competent money management personality—and you know what to look for!

33)

Successful "goal setting"—whether immediate, short, intermediate, or long term—begins inside your mind.

Because **"goal setting"** is a process it requires a mental planning stage on your part and a <u>written plan</u> thereafter—for the plan to be the most effective--and it is you who must implement and monitor your plan.

34)

Successful <u>"goal setting"</u> is a requirement if you truly want to reach your goals. You must be as specific and detailed as possible when setting your goals.

No amount of planning. whether detailed or not will be effective if you do not have the <u>will,</u> <u>desire</u> and <u>resources</u> to effectively <u>reach your goals</u> in the time frame designated in your <u>written plan.</u>

35)

It is imperative that you set up or establish a system within your mind of how to effectively manage your credit and finances in a manner that will ensure long term success—in today's economy!

You need a system that not only gives you the <u>clear credit and financial focus that you need and deserve</u>—you need a system that allows you to take your credit and finances as high as you choose <u>and will help you get to where</u>

you need or want to go, as you manage your cash flow!

36)

In order to gain the **foundation** that you need, you may have to do things in a different manner than you may have done in your past—if you desire to attain real success!

You must put together a written plan for the success that you desire and your clarity or vision of your future will come into clearer focus if you do it properly.

37)

By obtaining **a strong foundation** you will move forward in an effective manner and you will retain (mental working knowledge) in your mind what it takes to succeed on a daily basis with your credit and finances!

By having a strong foundation <u>you will contemplate your and your family's future in a serious manner!</u>

A **strong foundation** is absolutely necessary in the times that we now live in because <u>scammers</u> and others who are not out to benefit you—are all around you!

38)

You can now <u>reduce the anxiety</u> in your life by properly having the desire to use your mind and heart in a manner that really serves your and your family's best interest!

You can now gain the solid credit and financial foundation and focus that you need to succeed in today's economy—if you now have the mindset to pursue what is in your best interest!

39)

Always remember that by building your credit and financial foundation the right way, you are setting yourself and your family up for lasting success!

If you build your credit and financial foundation the wrong way—you are building a foundation that may look solid to your eyes—however, it will be a foundation that won't last!

40)

The <u>self-control</u> and <u>personal commitment</u> that is needed <u>must come from within you</u> if you are sincere **in making your dreams come true!**

You must have a yearning to create a **solid foundation** within your mind and heart if you truly desire to set yourself apart!

41)

Did you know that **how high you can go** with your credit and finances is in large part dependent upon **how strong your credit and financial foundation is?**

Always remember that the **base of operation** for major financial success **starts at your foundation!**

A faulty or non-existent foundation will not take you to where you need or desire to go!

42)

How you speak, feel and act toward yourself will play a large part in your future financial success. Always talk positively, feel good, and act in a manner that say's "I am a winner" <u>and even if you are not now a winner, you soon will be!</u>

In short, your **mental focus** on a daily basis plays a large part in your personal financial success—both now and in the future.

43)

Use your <u>mental focus</u> to be the best that you can be. You are in total control of your mind and <u>daily thoughts</u> and you can use that control to be the best "you" that "you" can be and your future can be as bright as <u>the stars up above that you see!</u>

Your mental focus must abound in you or control your daily thought process. Once that occurs you will begin to see positive movement in your finances and daily life!

44)

You must always "add to" your faith, preparation, and success to be even more successful. You should never be content at the level that you are currently at. Life is a continuum, and you can always do better in all areas of your life.

In the area of your personal finances your goal should be to structure your financial life in a manner that minimizes your financial stresses and **maximizes your financial well-being or positive thought process** about your current and future finances.

45)

You must be in total control of your financial life. You must not float along and be pulled in different directions by "MURPHY."

You must know that you have a bright and prosperous future—and it will show in your daily behavior and the way that you approach life.

Your goal is to have an inner peace within that cannot be shaken—and it will be largely due to the "choices" that you make from this day forward.

You must know that by using **"written goal setting"** you will see your future in <u>clear terms</u>—and your <u>focus will be magnified</u>—and your <u>dreams can actually be "brought to life."</u>

46)

If you take action and apply what you are learning at your highest level—and in a <u>sincere manner</u>—**you will have no reason or excuse** for not reaching your and your family's future goals.

You must act today, as by doing so a brighter future can be on the way!

You no longer have an excuse—if you act now—and put your mind to good use!

47)

You must have experiences in your life on a daily basis that provokes laughter and will cause you to <u>move forward in a manner where distractions will not have a major effect upon you</u> <u>and your family.</u>

By having a "keen sense of humor" you can move about through life in a more fluid manner and you can get <u>positive momentum</u> to work for you and not get down when adversity works against you!

48)

You must realize that adversity on multiple fronts may occur during your lifetime <u>in order to give you the added strength that you need</u> to succeed—**BIG TIME!**

You must look at what you are now facing as resistance—so that you will have the <u>strength and faith</u> later on that will lead to perseverance!

49)

Your challenge is remaining positive and continuing to do what is right and will move you forward when difficult times come!

You must know that by responding in a positive manner a much greater benefit is in your and your family's future.

In the long run <u>you must realize that adversity is actually developing you,</u> if you believe it to be true!

50)

By responding positively to adversity you will know <u>what lies in your future</u> and you will begin to <u>take the necessary action</u> that will lead to the success that you desire.

You will then look back in amazement at how <u>you once made the choice</u> to allow <u>anxiety to rule your life</u> for the period in your life that you allowed it to rule!

51)

It is important that you do the right thing for the right reason. It is important that you are intentional in what you do and the opportunity to do more in your life is now in front of you.

Don't let your current level of anxiety or fear limit your ability to dream big! Address what is trying to counteract or prevent you from achieving more in your life.

You are good enough; you can maintain all that you achieve—if you believe it to be true! However, by having a proactive approach and knowing the magnitude of what you need to do financially, you can achieve magnificent results and make the big dreams that you have blossom or come to life!

52)

You were placed on earth to work and create something new and meaningful (your life purpose) and to be a blessing for others and you can now do so by **using humor** and **other positive qualities of success** to assist you along the way!

It is important that you engage in laughter on a routine basis, so that you are more relaxed as you run your financial races!

53)

By starting on your financial path today—you must use humor and believe major success is ahead for you and your family—in a major way!

The question is—will you stay, or will you delay as far as putting together a plan so that success can go your way?

Success is already within you—what are you now going to do?

Be sure to use **humo**r as you move forward to make your and your family's dreams come true!

54)

Consistency allows you to know where you are going and will help provide you the determination that you need to get there!

Do you know what your goals and objectives are, and do you have a plan for achieving them? How can you attack your credit and finances more effectively?

You **must have a system** that allows you to operate effectively in your daily finances on a **consistent** basis.

By consistently doing what is necessary daily you put your heart and mind in position to achieve what you desire!

You now have a chance to learn what you need to do daily to attain **consistent** success!

The opportunity for you to achieve success on a **constant basis** is now in front of you!

Are you at this time determined to do what you need to do? You must realize that to succeed **consistently**—it may require the cooperation of others—no successful person is an island onto himself!

55)

It is important that you focus on the important areas of your credit and finances so that you can gain a powerful advantage that will move you forward in an effective and efficient manner!

If you consistently do what you were put on earth to do—you can make your dreams come true!

You can never fail consistently if you decide to get up **consistently** and pursue success **consistently!**

By **consistently** <u>looking inside yourself and improving on qualities or areas that you are weakest in</u>—your stronger qualities will be greatly enhanced!

56)

It is better to stay ahead of the curve than behind the curve! Did you know that to operate more effectively and efficiently—it requires **consistent action** on your part?

You must meet success head on and expect a collision with it—because success won't expect to find you and collide with you—if you don't do what you need to do!

You must realize that your consistent comprehension alone is not enough. It is what you do with what you comprehend, and what

you do with the knowledge that you will gain that really counts!

You must realize that in most cases, something for nothing is usually worth nothing!

Don't get too excited about temporary success! You must diligently seek success on a permanent basis and put forward the required effort on a **consistent** basis!

57)

Your success consciousness can be enhanced by learning the appropriate "success principles."

What quality and quantity of service do you provide to others on a **consistent** basis? The quality and quantity of service that you provide will determine in large part how successful you will be in your future!

58)

If you earn consistently and save consistently you can start on a path to the success that you desire!

You must get to a point where the small voice within you that you hear—speaks success—and you must expect nothing less than success **on a consistent basis!**

How high will you decide to go after you have faced great adversity? By having the right mindset, you can reach a higher level of success!

The longer your **consistent thought patterns** are—the greater your future success can be! What **you do consistently** determines in large part where you will go and how high you can take your success!

Are you happy where you are? Are you happy where you are going?

They are really one in the same! Once you line up your mind and heart with the goals that you desire to achieve—you make success much more likely to occur!

Your daily action determines your present and future success!

What are your aspirations? Do you desire financial freedom or just comfortable living—car—house—money in bank etcetera. Or, do you desire to leave a lasting legacy for your family and/or society?

Your **persistent and consistent** use of this this book can provide you and your family—a new look!

59)

By **dreaming big** and taking "consistent" **decisive action** the **mental focus** that is needed along with the **determination** and **personal commitment** that is needed can come forth in a powerful manner!

Imagine yourself not listening to naysayers and others who might try to persuade you in the opposite direction of your big dream!

Imagine if you unrelentingly pursue what is due to you in a manner that truly served your best interest!

Imagine if you could go out and actually do what you were put on earth to!

60)

You must realize that by **dreaming big** you provide the catalyst for real change that can make a real difference in your life. However, you must realize that it will take <u>preparation on your part</u> if you truly desire to bring your "big dream" into reality!

You must know that it will take preparation and effort on your part if you desire to bring into reality the big goals that now reside in your heart.

61)

You must have the <u>"preparation"</u> that is needed if you desire to bring **your big dream** into reality—whether it be improving your credit and finances to a high level or any other goal **or dream** that you may have in mind!
You must also realize that <u>you must be resilient</u> and <u>diligent</u> and never quit <u>as adversity and other happenings that may cause stress in your life</u> will

occur as you move toward your "big dream!"

62)

You must realize that you will have to **"take action"** to make your dream occur! You can't just have faith that it will happen and not actively work **to make it happen.**

However, you must realize that if you stay committed and do the work that is necessary you can make your **"big dream"** happen!

63)

Always realize that if you don't have an **imaginative spirit**—it can be cultivated over time. Daily meditation along with regular exercise can do wonders for **your imagination** and help you be a better person.

You can improve your focus and get to the point where you want to improve your life in all areas—including your credit and finances.

You can gain the **preparation** that you need—to succeed.

64)

By focusing on what is important and gaining the **preparation that is needed** you can move forward in an effective manner and you will increase your **imaginative thoughts** (you start to dream big) and you will start to believe that you can **attain goals** that you never thought possible.

If you "focus in" at the right time in your life **you can accomplish many goals that you may have thought were out of reach for you and your family.**

65)

Use **your imagination to dream big** and follow your dream with a written plan to make it happen. Be sure to use **goal setting** along with proven systems to make your and your family's dream a reality—starting today!

You now know that you must reach higher and you now know that "preparation" is a key component for reaching the success that you desire!

66)

Always remember that when you are in the process of improving your credit and finances **you must dream big** and you must use your **imaginative** <u>thoughts</u> in a manner that serves your and your family's best interest!

And always remember that there are no limits on what you can do if you don't set any limits!

If you set limits, you not only limit what you can do, you put in motion the mental processes to not make your dreams come true!

67)

By properly utilizing a **<u>personal cash flow statement</u>** prior to purchasing and/or selling your home you can better determine if home ownership is appropriate for you at this time, or whether staying where you are and saving—and/or pursuing other options are your best choice.

A personal cash flow statement helps determine how liquid you are and is a good barometer in determining your ability to meet your future financial obligations.

By creating a personal cash flow before your major purchases, you can use it as a tool to plan for more success in your future.

68)

The balance sheet is a listing of assets, liabilities, and net worth that outlines your resources and shows how those resources were obtained or financed.

The **balance sheet statement** is a particular snapshot of your finances at a **particular point in time** (the date of the statement). Many third parties (Banks, Lenders etc.) utilized the **personal balance sheet** in the past when deciding to grant certain credit.

A balance sheet allows you to know if your finances are in balance and can guide you as you build your net worth.

69)

A **personal balance sheet** will give you a good idea of your financial condition if you are organized and **want to totally take control of your finances.**

A Personal Balance Sheet Statement will show you whether you hit your targeted goals and show you if you fell short as it will outline your assets, liabilities, and net worth.

70)

Your "Net Worth Statement" is a much better metric than simply what your income is or what you appear to own and appear to owe.

Your annual goal should always be to increase your net worth!

<u>A major factor in increasing your net worth is the proper buying and selling of your home and managing your finances effectively in a comprehensive manner.</u>

71)

By **knowing your financial situation** "up front" <u>you can plan for your future more effectively</u> and get a realistic picture of how <u>you can enjoy life</u> and get the pleasures of life that you know you deserve.

You must be engaged with your finances and not enraged by the status of your finances!

Also, by knowing your financial position after your home purchase **(by doing this analysis on the front end)** you will know your financial situation after your projected home purchase and/or sale.

72)

In a nutshell, **personal financial statements** can help you plan better when you have adequate financial information in **easy-to-understand statements.**

The financial statements—however—are only as good as the accuracy of the data inputted.

Therefore, you want to be sure that your income and expenses are as accurate as possible, and your assets and liabilities are as accurate as possible to maximize your opportunity for success.

73)

Always remember that
personal financial statements are an aid
to sound financial management and not
a substitute for <u>sound financial
management.</u>

"The <u>real key</u> is do you have the <u>proper
motivation inside</u> to apply the
information derived from the **financial
analysis** to move in the **<u>right direction</u>** to
improve your life and that of your
family's?"

By properly creating **personal financial
statements** and applying the information
properly it will benefit you and your
family the most!

74)

The <u>sharing of helpful knowledge</u> to really benefit others should be high on your priority list.

If you possess a high level of **"knowledge"** that can truly benefit others in a helpful and meaningful way, it is important that you have a sharing spirit.

By having a sharing spirit, you are showing that you get it—and the success that you desire will be attained—bit by bit!

75)

Don't watch <u>opportunity</u> and life pass you by! You must decide to give it your best and create an effective plan for your future credit and financial success!

Be sure to <u>move to action</u>—you now have access to powerful credit and finance improvement advice and information that can transform your current situation!

76)

You must remember that you possess the power within <u>to create</u> <u>wealth,</u> <u>create opportunity</u> and <u>change</u> <u>who you are!</u>

The knowledge of how to effectively transform your credit and financial future in a meaningful way can be found inside of you if you take the right action.

You must realize that it will take <u>effort on your part</u> to apply empowering information in an effective manner— nothing of "real value" will be given to you!

77)

It is important that you discover what you are passionate about and use your ideas <u>to make great things happen in your life!</u>

You are <u>responsible</u> for your and your family's success!

You must have the courage to pursue your future goals with <u>laser like focus</u> and a <u>high level of determination if you truly desire to improve your situation.</u>

78)

You must pursue the <u>right knowledge</u> to move yourself and your family forward at a steady and successful pace.

Be sure to learn what you need to learn and apply the information that you feel can effectively move you and your family forward in an effective manner!

You don't have to let worry enter your thought process. You must <u>control your own thoughts</u> and operate at a high level of <u>confidence</u> when it comes to your future.

79)

You must always live your life in a manner where your "dominant thoughts" are always positive!

By utilizing <u>effective planning</u> and focusing on the positive—success will be in your future.

You must have the "right knowledge" inside of your mind for your mind to produce the results that you desire for yourself and your family!

80)

Do you currently have the "right knowledge" that is necessary to ensure the future success that you desire for yourself and your family?

If you don't—there is no need to panic!

You must realize that Math and English are taught for a number of years during your educational years!

You must realize that Personal Finance and Economics—that you often use much more frequently in your adult life are rarely taught during your educational years!

Even so, it is your responsibility to obtain the knowledge that you need—to succeed.

81)

You can now learn what you need to learn at your leisure and apply powerful systems and concepts that can move you towards the goals that serve your and your family's best interest!

By having the "right knowledge"—you put yourself in position to <u>see success in your mind</u> and then <u>pursue that</u>

success with the **real expectation that it will happen!**

Use the knowledge that you have gained to truly transform your and your family's credit and financial future!

You and your family should have it no other way!

82)

You must be **prepared** for your credit and financial journey if your goal is to improve the living conditions for yourself and your family to a high level.
Obtaining the "know how" of how to successfully reach your future credit and financial goals takes **"preparation"** on your part.

If you have bad knowledge in your

understanding of your credit and finances—you will have bad judgment in most cases.

83)

The first part of **"preparation"** in reaching your credit and financial goals are to understand that you <u>must obtain the knowledge that is necessary</u> for you to effectively manage and improve your credit and finances. It is important that you are <u>committed at a high level </u>to reach your <u>goals.</u>

You must know (within your own mind) whether you are truly committed to reaching your goals.

Proper preparation in many cases takes time and effort and if you lack the <u>commitment that is necessary</u> to

"prepare yourself" for a successful financial future—you may not reach your goals.

By obtaining the **"knowledge" that is necessary** to really move yourself and your family forward you put yourself and your family in position for future success in a more **efficient manner!**

84)

Being **prepared on the front end** prior to putting your credit and financial improvement plan in place is a critical component of you truly reaching your and your family's financial goals and objectives in an effective manner.

Unlike many, by **preparing for your future success** "prior to" starting on your credit and finance journey—you will put yourself and your family in "real position" to make "real success" a "real possibility!"

By properly **"preparing in advance"** you are showing that you are "sincere" in reaching your and your family's future credit and financial goals.

85)

By taking the time now to really "properly prepare" yourself for your financial future you are making a good choice and future success at a "high level" will be in your and your family's future!

You must be a knower, doer and believer—if you want to be a high

achiever!

Improving your personal finances to a high level requires that you know what you must do prior to starting on your credit and finance journey.

86)

In other areas where you obtain a vision to pursue a goal or reach your life purpose you may not have clear knowledge of how you will accomplish your vision—but it will come to you as you act.

Improving your credit and finances differs from other goals or objectives that you may have, because it is an area that offers a long track record of how to attain your goals successfully.

Find your goals and objectives that are most pressing to you and pursue your path to success!

87)

To improve your credit and finances to a high level you must gain all of the <u>right knowledge—prior to starting</u> on your financial journey.

Doing so will put you in position to make decisions that are good for you and your family!

You must then (apply) "do" what you "know" in a manner that will benefit you and your family the most.

88)

At all times <u>you must have faith</u> and "believe" and "know" that you really will achieve the goals and objectives that you set for yourself and your family.

By "knowing, doing and believing" at a high level—you put yourself in position to attain <u>"the success that you desire"</u> for yourself and your family!

89)

By properly **"preparing"** on the front end you are planting a seed in fertile ground <u>(deep inside your heart and mind)</u> and <u>your harvest will be bountiful</u>—if you <u>stay focused</u> on a consistent basis.

You must fully realize that proper preparation is the key to your credit and financial success!

90)

You must get into the habit of never obtaining your understanding and practical application of your credit and finance systems and approaches while you are in the middle of a transaction!

You must be **prepared** (<u>obtain the mental working knowledge</u>) on the front end if you want to pursue your goals properly (attain the success that is in your best interest) and in a manner that leads to true and lasting success!

91)

You must realize that you can't effectively develop a plan in the middle of your transaction—or on the fly!

If you are in the process of <u>improving your cash flow,</u> <u>improving your credit,</u> or <u>improving your finances</u> in any or all areas—you must have an <u>effective mental process</u> and clear <u>vision</u> of how you will get there!

92)

You must gain the <u>knowledge</u> and <u>practical application</u> that is necessary on the <u>front end</u> if you want to be more effective and really reach a high level of success!

By doing so you can benefit yourself and

your family in a way that can really provide you the _direction that you and your family need_!

By doing so you can _get on a path_ of success that will have fewer roadblocks and pitfalls—therefore you will be able to take your success to a very high level in a more efficient manner!

93)

Be sure to **prepare your mind** for the credit and finance journey that can lead to you living your life on your terms and in a manner that _gives you joy at a level that you desire_!

You must believe that you can do just that and by doing so you will attain success beyond _your imagination_!

94)

It is important that you do things in your credit and financial life in an orderly fashion—and it is important that you do what you <u>need to do!</u>

Speaking of orderly fashion—you must utilize personal finance statements appropriately, master your credit and manage all areas of your finances at an optimal level.

95)

To be truly successful you must gain the "<u>preparation</u>" that is needed on the front end so that your mind and heart is ready for what it is about to receive—as it relates to your credit and finances.

You must possess **"positive qualities of success"**—at an acceptable level—if you desire to get powerful results!

96)

You must possess in your mind the knowledge of what you need to do on a daily basis to work toward making your dreams come true.

Do you have a system that addresses what needs to be addressed?

Are you aware of how you can use personal financial statements effectively? Do you have a highly effective way of managing and improving your credit?

97)

Do you know <u>all of the areas</u> of your credit and finances that you must address and <u>do you have an effective system</u> of addressing those areas comprehensively?

Well, you need a system that does address those areas that need to be addressed <u>and you need a system that "you" possess—within your mind</u>—that provides you the knowledge and ability to address those areas.

98)

You must have a mindset that states—<u>I will take action</u> and **<u>do what is necessary</u>** to reach <u>all of the goals</u> that I desire.

You must get to a point where taking the right action is almost like a reflex action—you don't even have to think about it—<u>you take the right action in a manner that is natural</u>—that becomes the norm for you—even though it might not be the norm for others.

99)

Preparation helps you to gain an <u>"active mindset"</u> that allows you to apply the knowledge that you have in a more effective manner—than if you did not prepare your mind on the front end.

100)

You must have a system that allows you to look at what you have done—determine if you are on track to get the desired results or get the desired results and move forward from there with confidence and in a manner that makes sense.

101)

If you see areas that can be improved, or you see results that are not to your liking—you want to be in position to make the necessary adjustments and move forward from there.

MONTOR RESULTS—and make improvements on a consistent basis.

102)

Who will you join as far as your wealth building style?

Those who learn how to do it the right way through suffering (making mistakes and learning from those mistakes and correcting their future behavior).

Those who suffer over and over because they don't learn from their mistakes (they lack wisdom).

Those who avoid suffering by <u>learning how to do it the right way on the front end</u>—or they **learn from the mistakes of others** (wisdom is at work here).

103)

*You must **make it a priority** to <u>equip your mind </u>with the knowledge that is needed to manage your finances effectively on a consistent basis!*

You must make it a priority to learn in a clear and concise way if <u>your investments that you currently have (or</u>

will eventually have) are invested in a tax-efficient—or tax inefficient manner—and use that knowledge **right now** to possibly reduce your taxes—and enhance your future earnings!

104)

You can now educate yourself efficiently and effectively in any and all areas of your personal finances—if you choose to do so!

You must not take generic or bad advice that you may receive (including advice from this book) and not analyze what you receive in an **analytical, accurate, careful and critical** manner.

You must be intelligent in your approach to understanding any advice that you may receive that you plan on applying to your—or your family's situation!

105)

Always realize that there are some things in life that you can't understand fully unless you have been through that situation—<u>however mismanaging your credit and finances</u>—does not have to be one of those situations!

You must be active in ensuring your future success. <u>That means continually preparing your mind for success by obtaining the right knowledge</u> and applying that knowledge in the most effective manner possible.

106)

You must ensure that you are getting the desired results, or you are on track to doing so in a time efficient manner— otherwise a change in strategy or approach may be needed.

By doing all the above consistently—you will put yourself and your family on an upward trend towards long-term success that will allow you to live your life in a style and manner that serves your and your family's best long-term interest.

107)

*By **prioritizing** the work that you need to do in your credit and financial life, <u>you gain clarity</u> and you increase the odds of a successful outcome.*

The payoff of all of your creditors can occur, purchasing your dream home can occur, living your retirement in abundance can occur, leaving an inheritance for your kids and grand-kids can occur—however, <u>it all starts inside of you</u>—as you must do what you need to do!

108)

By **prioritizing** your financial steps <u>you can put yourself in position to make your future happen</u>—instead of merely just waiting on it to happen.

Many consumers wait on success to happen—and often end up transitioning before they reach their significant goals—don't let that be you! Act now and work toward making your dreams come true!

By <u>actively doing</u> what you need to do, you put yourself and your family in position for success.

109)

Even if the success that you desire may not occur when you want it to occur, you must realize that by **prioritizing your steps**—the success that you desire will occur in a more efficient and lasting manner.

It is important that you prepare your mind with the right knowledge and take that knowledge that you possess and to make the future success that you desire occur—**<u>Right Now!</u>**

110)

When you learn new material or material for the first time that is presented in a boring or traditional format it is not uncommon for you to understand the material at the time that you read the material—or even a few days afterwards.

However, after that the information is often forgotten and will have no real meaning in your life.

The material will in many cases not have any relevance to your life, or move to the farther recesses of your mind due to lack of importance or other factors in your own mind.

Isn't it time you get boredom out of your life?

111)

When you learn new material or material that is presented in a different or non-traditional format it is not uncommon for you to "process" the information differently due in large part to the way that the information is presented.

By processing the information in a different manner your understanding of the material in many cases will be deeper at the time and "if the information is really meaningful to you and your family" you will be able to understand and apply the information effectively even a few months—and possibly years afterwards.

112)

By learning **new information** effectively, the information will in many cases **remain in your heart and mind and become a permanent fixture in your thought process** on a consistent basis if you obtain the mental working knowledge that is required!

Furthermore, if you receive "high value information" that has real meaning to you and your life that is written in a style that you can readily comprehend, you will often become determined and motivated to **mentally grasp that information** and use it to improve your and your family's living conditions.

113)

By receiving the right type of information, you can more easily "mentally grasp" the information and use it to improve your and your family's living conditions in a much more effective manner.

Furthermore, in this high tech and fast moving environment that we now live in, you must be able to process and apply information in an efficient and effective manner and it is the goal of <u>this book</u> to provide tools that will allow you to do just that.

114)

It is important that you learn "high value information" that is of the kind that you can <u>readily grasp</u>, has meaning to you and your family and above all **will move you and your family "forward"** in your credit, finance and any other area of your life that is important to you.

By having the right "mental working knowledge" you will put yourself in real position to change the course of your future in a real and meaningful way!

You will have the power within your own mind to take initiative and move forward on matters of importance in your and your family's life!

115)

If you truly desire future success, you will aspire to obtain the **"mental working knowledge"** that is needed for success in your everyday life.

You can put yourself in position to achieve untold success in your future and you can make a <u>sincere effort</u> to use the "mental working knowledge" that is needed for success in your life in a more appropriate manner.

116)

Many consumers often overlook the amount of **self-discipline** (or doing what needs to be done) when they begin their financial planning.

You must understand that it is difficult to do what needs to be done on a daily, weekly, monthly, and yearly basis to improve your finances to a high level.

However, by properly processing what you are learning you can gain the <u>mental fortitude</u> that you need to succeed!

In today's society there is a high amount of "noise" and "distractions" at every turn and you want to maintain the proper focus.

117)

You will face challenges in your life daily, from family to friends to entertainment, to trying to keep up with what others are doing, to everyday stress and the like.

To have the proper focus and **self-discipline** that is required for success in this day and age will truly set you apart from your peers and society in general.

You must not let the distractions in your life negatively affect your credit and financial future!

118)

Even though **self-discipline** and properly focusing over a period of time is difficult for many—you now have an opportunity to improve in those areas and achieve what you desire!

You must realize that with "popular" society the norm—what is now being pushed is instant gratification and satisfaction.

*In some areas of your life, you must display **self-discipline** now—to achieve what you "really" desire and deserve—later!*

119)

Those who have the mental focus and self-discipline to achieve their goals and

life objectives will normally achieve success if they pursue their dreams at a high level and they stay focused and disciplined!

You too, can achieve the **self-discipline** that is needed to reach your goals if you sincerely make the decision to do so and you then cultivate the habits that are necessary in a determined manner and you remain focused!

120)

You must get into a habit of doing what you say you will do!

You must get to a point where you can set a goal, no matter how small and actually pursue and achieve that goal.

That will then give you the <u>confidence</u> that you need and if you continue to set and reach your goals consistently you will develop the **habit of self-discipline** that is required in your financial and other areas of your life.

121)

You must have the real belief that you can achieve your <u>retirement goals,</u> <u>pay off your debt in a timely manner,</u> <u>save for your children's education</u> in an efficient manner or reach any other <u>goal or objective</u> that you may have for yourself and your family.

If your goal is to effectively utilize "self-discipline" in your life, you must develop a track record of doing what you say you will do over a period of time!

122)

In the times that we now live in it is absolutely imperative that you have **self-discipline** and <u>mental focus</u> at all times!

By doing so you will put yourself and your family on a path to financial and life success.

Cultivating the habit of **self-discipline** will undoubtedly play a major role in your and your family's financial future. Use the knowledge of why having **self-discipline** at a high level <u>is a major key</u> in reaching your and your family's goals.

123)

If your goal is to effectively utilize "self-discipline" in your life, you must develop a track record of doing what you say you will do. By properly utilizing **self-discipline**—success is <u>within your and your family's grasps.</u>

What Are the Benefits of Self-discipline?

Do you know what you value?

If you are **disciplined** in your daily activities you will <u>move diligently towards your goals</u> and you will have a <u>less stressful lifestyle!</u> To apply **discipline** daily you must have courage, <u>as fear is not a part of self-discipline.</u>

124)

Discipline forces you to have self-control! Do you, have it? Can you put a plan in place and stick to it?

By cultivating **discipline** at a high level you will build your character. If you live aimlessly and have no plan of action, you will in most cases be **living a stressful life.**

125)

By utilizing **discipline** effectively, you will begin to feel good about yourself and your financial future.

It takes **self-discipline** to do what is right for your financial future.

You want to comprehend what you are learning at your highest level and apply what you feel can move you and your family forward so that you can reach your highest level of potential?

Even if you are highly talented at what you do—that alone is not enough if you desire to reach a <u>higher level of excellence</u>!

126)

Did you know that self-discipline is a choice that you make?

Those who are **disciplined** in one area are often **disciplined** in other areas of their life as well—whether it be their health, eating habits, impact on others (enthusiasm) and their daily habits.

Those who display **self-discipline** consistently know that they are going somewhere (and others know too) because they are disciplined in their approach in many areas of their life!

127)

This book came into existence by having self-discipline and in large part by **self-discipline** being applied on a consistent basis. Use the self-discipline that you now have or will soon have to do more in your life

By being **disciplined** others will see in you—your success qualities.

You must realize that you may have to work on improving your **self-discipline** in a determined manner! You must never give up!

By doing so you can create and open up new opportunities for success in all areas of your life!

128)

You must decide to <u>take action daily</u> and in a <u>timely manner</u> on all matters of significance in your and your family's life.

You must know <u>"what to take action on"</u> daily by gaining the <u>preparation</u> and <u>knowledge</u> that is needed so that you can <u>achieve the success that you desire.</u>

You must comprehend and apply the <u>"success principles"</u> on a consistent basis.

129)

You must have the mindset that you will be <u>diligent in all that you do</u> and you must have the mindset that you will <u>excel at your highest level</u> in all that you do.

By obtaining the self-discipline that you need to succeed—you are showing that you have the <u>staying power or endurance</u> that is needed for success in today's economy or any economy and success will be more likely to come to you, because you decided in a sincere way to do what you need to do.

130)

It is particularly important in the times that we now live in that you live your life with "high standards" as a major benchmark in your life.

Even if you are currently very successful in your credit and financial life you need to <u>operate from the perspective</u> that the success that you now enjoy can be improved. You should want to take your success to a higher state!

Even though you may appear successful in your own eyes and in the eyes of others, there is always room for improvement.

However, you and your family should be commended for reaching your current level of success and you must continue to give it your best.

131)

You are showing that you have the strength to encounter and <u>overcome from any adversity</u> that you may face.

You are showing that you have the <u>"know how"</u> of how to achieve in this economy—when others have the me-me-me—now-now-now attitude!

Your <u>outlook on your future</u> will improve because you now know that you have the **<u>discipline within you</u>—<u>to make your dreams come true!</u>**

132)

If you try to excel in all areas of your credit, financial and everyday life, <u>you bring the possibility</u> for increased success in your and your family's life.

You must make the decision to excel at your highest level as you improve your credit, finance, and real estate pursuits.

You must see the wisdom in selecting the best information that you use to change your future in a major way, or you will remain where you are currently at or move forward at a slow pace!

133)

You must make it a point to **operate at a high level of excellence** in all that you do if <u>your goal is to be successful at a very high level.</u>

You must set the bar high and reach higher in your life!

Make it a point at this time to do your absolute best at <u>what you are doing </u>or plan to do!

You can't <u>depend on others</u> to take you to where you need or want to be.

134)

If you are in the process of improving your credit and finances, you want to do your absolute best at attaining those goals!

You must have the attitude that you will **excel at your highest level** while you are on <u>your journey to reaching your goals</u> for yourself and your family.

It is important that you are <u>"properly prepared"</u> and you have the <u>"proper focus"</u> if you want to **excel at a high level.**

Excellence and high standards are required if you want to reach your credit, financial and life goals!

135)

Don't live your life in a manner where you accept mediocrity and less than your best in all that you do!

Excellence is a quality that you must always aspire to attain!

You can have a successful, prosperous future if you **set your standards high** and you **operate at a high level of excellence** daily!

Be sure to <u>aim high</u>, <u>have meaningful and beneficial goals for yourself and your family</u> and **<u>do your best to excel</u>** in all that you engage in.

136)

Your **personal standards** should be at such a high level that nothing that the outside world will say or do—will affect you in a negative way!

Quite the contrary, negative comments by others should give you a high level of <u>inspiration</u> and <u>motivation!</u>

Now <u>is the time</u> to ask **Why!** Now is the Time to set the bar **High!** By doing so <u>You can exceed the **Sky!**</u>

137)

Be sure to set meaningful and inspiring goals and do your absolute best to reach those goals.

You must set the bar high if you are to exceed the sky!

You must reach down in your soul— muster up the strength to reach your goal—and know that success in all that you do will be a lifetime role!

Go out and make your dreams come true as there are many routes that provides you a road map of what you can <u>NOW </u>do—to see your way through!

138)

It is important that you have a strong and healthy view of yourself and your financial future.

You must feel that you not only deserve a successful future—you must know and understand that it is your birthright.

You were created to do great things in your life and now is the time that you <u>live up to those expectations.</u>

139)

You were put on earth to create the future that you desire and to advance society!

From this point forward you must stop doing less than your best and <u>elevate your mind to a high level</u> so that you can do great things while you are here on earth!

You must make a conscious decision to feel good about yourself, your family, and your financial future!

140)

No one can make you look at yourself and feel good about yourself—you must do it!

Regardless of <u>how others look at themselves and their situation,</u> you must have a **positive view of your future** and the success that you will create!

You must know and understand your purpose for being here at this time and you must feel **worthy of living** in your purpose!

141)

You must know that you can create the future that you desire, and you should feel good about having the knowledge that you can create the future that you desire.

It is important that you realize that your happiness and **self-worth** must come from within you!

*You cannot expect to receive your happiness and **self-worth** from others or your material possessions.*

142)

If you improve your credit and finances to a high level—doing so could provide you the freedom to do the things in life that you really enjoy, thus increasing your happiness and the way that you feel about yourself on a daily basis.

You must **feel good about yourself** and you must have a high level of self-esteem towards yourself and <u>confidence</u> in your financial future.

You must realize that your starting point for your happiness and self-worth is inside of your mind and heart!

143)

You can use your conscious mind to <u>make the decision</u> to improve in all areas of your life by making the decision to do so and then following through on that decision with <u>decisive action!</u>

Improving your credit and finances and **simplifying your financial life** can lead to you feeling better about yourself.

Doing so on a consistent basis can lead to you living a happy and meaningful life—**<u>where joy is at the center!</u>**

144)

You cannot do like some who live their life in <u>uncertainty</u> and yet believe they will accomplish their dreams (goals).

You must "know and receive" your dreams (goals)—because you have a <u>written plan of action</u> in place and a <u>high level of faith </u>about your future that cannot be shaken!

You must know within your mind and heart that you can accomplish any goal that you set!

145)

The key to your success may be that you must put your <u>goals and dreams in writing</u> and <u>create a workable plan to make your goals and dreams a reality.</u>

If you believe success lives in you, success will believe in you.

*You must feel **worthy** of all the **success that is in your future!***

When proper preparation, know-how, execution and faith meet inside of your mind and heart—"success" will say— WELCOME!

146)

You have all that it takes inside of you to reach great heights in your life!

Now is the time that you make a serious move and pursue the greatness that lies inside of you. You are **truly worth** what you were put on earth to do.

Live out **your purpose for being here** in the most enthusiastic and beneficial way possible. You and your family should have it no other way!

147)

Always remember that you have the "power" to take your mind to a <u>"good place!"</u>

You don't have to stay in a <u>"low place"</u> if you <u>make the choice</u> not too.

Make the decision right now to feel good about yourself, your future, and the actions that you will take daily!

148)

You are worthy of whatever you decide in your mind that you are worthy of,

and your lack of action daily will speak volumes!

On the flip side, your decision and follow through on taking decisive action daily will also speak volumes!

Always remember that many can quote wise thoughts, however very few can apply wise thoughts effectively and in a manner that can transform their life.

149)

You can aim high or aim low! No one else can control your aim!

__You__ control how you feel about yourself and the direction that your life will take!

Use that knowledge to control your future and stop blaming others or let how others look at you and feel about you affect your life in a detrimental way!

Use that knowledge to free your mind from anything in your past or your family's past that may be holding you back from reaching your goals!

150)

You have the <u>mental capacity</u> to do great things in your life—you don't have to live your life in strife!

It is important that you be all that "you" can be, and you reach toward the stars and go as higher than you can see!

151)

Greatness is in You (Give It Your All)

No one can see what you see or do what you do.

You are a unique creation the world is waiting on you!

Your gifts and talents can be seen all around.

Please don't let us down!

We want to ensure that your gifts are around.

Will you do (be) all that you can and not let us down!

Your gifts and talents are our reward.

For you not to give it your all would not lead us forward.

Use your creativity and not negativity—
you'll receive a positive charge and go
down in history—as large.

Is it any wonder that you have what it
takes?

You can be all that you want to be if you
don't put on the brakes!

Do you know that you are great?

Provide us your gift (purpose) for being
here—the world can no longer wait!

Do you know that you have the strength
that you need—to succeed?

Greatness is in you—you can make all
your dreams come true!

Starting today—will you do what you
need to do?

152)

Give serious thought to the future that you desire and use your <u>focus</u> along with <u>the pages on this site</u> to truly transform your and your family's future!

You have the power to "break free" from your past and forge a great future for yourself and your family—starting today!

You must realize that hope, wishful thinking or prayer—**<u>without action</u>** is not a strategy.

153)

You must know that major success can be in your and your family's future <u>by taking appropriate action</u> and doing what you need to do on a consistent basis!

Putting a <u>plan in action</u> that is measurable and has definite deadlines for achievement is a strategy—if done properly!

You can <u>demonstrate faith</u> and the fact that you value your and your family's future by <u>taking action at a high level</u> and <u>achieving at a high level</u>—right now!

154)

You and your family are **worthy** of a prosperous and successful future! Now is the time that you <u>affirm that reality!</u>

It is important that you speak in a "voice" that is totally unique and original—and you must feel worthy of your **life purpose** or the **assignment that you have** in your life. **Whether you are facing adversity or moving along at a** good and prosperous pace, you must encourage yourself and achieve positive results as you move along in life.

155)

By having faith that you can achieve your goals you can change your life and the direction that you are going—right now!

The key to your success is how you "comprehend" and "utilize (apply) the knowledge" that you will gain in your daily life.

It is important that you **engage your heart and mind at your highest level** and you **use your willpower to take the appropriate action** that you need to take on a consistent basis.

156)

If you don't act now—do you really have faith that you will have a successful future in the area of your choosing?

When it comes to **self-worth** you must always **believe that you are worthy of a prosperous and successful future.**

You must use your imagination and say to yourself—**why not me**, particularly if there is something big that **you really want to do!**

157)

You must realize that you can't wait on others to tell you that it is OK to create what you desire to make a reality!

It will not be an accident when you create something that is totally original and presented in a way that only you could create.

When you are **original in what you do** you will be rewarded beyond your imagination and you will put yourself in position to exponentially expand your thought horizon!

158)

By being original, you can put yourself in position to come up with new and highly creative ways of doing things— regardless of your life purpose.

By being totally original you can create something new, forward moving and exciting for those who are empowered by what you create.

159)

By being original in your approach, <u>thoughts at a high level</u> will be in your midst on a consistent basis and if you <u>act on those thoughts</u> in a meaningful way— you can take your life in the direction of your life purpose.

In this book you will find original thoughts on original pages on virtually every page in this book and that is no accident!

You must act on <u>inspiration</u> that comes from within and you must feel that **you are worthy** of the success that you desire, regardless of the area that you decide to excel in.

160)

Do you know that you are worthy of whatever you think you are worthy of? Do you know your purpose for your life at this time?

Answer the above questions appropriately and use that knowledge to reach your highest heights as you move towards the success that you desire for yourself and your family!

It is important that you realize from this day forward that as it relates to your and your family's future success—your **self-worth** is far more important than your **net worth.**

161)

Now is the time to go after what you see—if it is in your best interest to do so!

It is very important that **you feel worthy of the success that can truly be yours** if only you pursued what you really want out of life at a high level and you truly believe in your mind and heart that you will succeed.

You now know that **you are worthy of the success** that you now see or will soon see!

162)

Your **self-worth** or how you feel about yourself on a consistent basis is more important than your **net worth, how**

others feel about you or what you are worth from a <u>financial standpoint</u> at this time.

However, you don't have to shortchange yourself or your family either way!

By <u>learning what you need to learn</u> and applying what you feel can move you and your family forward <u>you can position yourself for success in a comprehensive way—starting today.</u>

163)

A you navigate life—always remember that **you are Worth—what you think you are WORTH!**

We wish you and your family untold success in the future!

164)

Isn't it time you learn of powerful success formulas that you can use to immediately increase the likelihood of success in your and your family's credit and financial life or any other area of your life that you desire success in.

First and foremost to achieve the success that you desire—you must have the <u>right mindset</u> or you must gain the <u>preparation</u> and <u>knowledge</u> that will put you in the right frame of mind to attain the success that you desire.

Now is the time that you pursue what you need to know in a more rigorous manner!

165)

You must feel worthy that you can attain the credit, finance, and real estate success that you desire in a more effective and efficient manner!

Whether debt pay off or debt pay down is your goal, <u>whether funding your retirement accounts at the right level is your goal</u>, whether leaving a lasting legacy for your family members is your goal—you can attain any and all of the goals that you desire if you open up your mind to the possibility!

166)

By comprehending at your highest level and then <u>applying what you feel will work</u> to bring you the success that you desire for yourself and your family—you can **win** in your financial life!

It is you who must determine and decide who your goals are and then you must have the mindset that you will achieve those goals!

167)

You have the potential to attain many of your goals, however "potential to do so" means that you have not done it!

You must be diligent in your approach as well as vigilant in your approach and you must be fully committed to achieving your goals at this time!

You must use the knowledge that you are learning as a "springboard toward success" so that you can go as high as you want or need to go.

168)

You can excel! You can come up and out of any situation that you are in if you have the <u>proper mindset!</u> You must be excellent in spirit and always move forward—**mediocre goals must not be a part of your mindset.**

If you diligently work toward your goals and you do not let <u>distractions negatively affect you</u>—you will gradually improve and success will occur, if you are consistent in your approach towards working toward your goal(s)!

169)

Pursuing excellence **(winning)** requires
focus of thought and the decision by you
to operate in excellence! It is the
intentional use of your mind to enhance
the probability of the outcome that you
desire.

Why You Must Have Winning Thoughts

You must ask yourself—what am I strong
in? Focus on your strength—you must
know what to focus on! You must do a
little extra to distinguish yourself from
the rest in your area of strength and
work harder to improve in your area of
weakness—if you truly desire to win!

170)

If you desire excellence to show up in the finished product, you must be consistent in your approach.

You must have positive thoughts! You must believe in yourself at a very high level and you must always get back up and make the best of your situation— NOW!

You must excel and you must move forward! You must focus daily, and you must get better! You must pay attention to the details! You must **plan for your success!**

171)

Do you have unfinished business in your life that you have been reluctant to *address? Now is the time that you act on a consistent basis **so that you can win!***

Your goal is to stretch your mind toward what is meaningful and significant to you so that you can reach higher and make what you really desire come true.

Why set mediocre goals that you may or may not achieve when you can reach higher and make what you desire a reality—if you truly believe!

172)

You want to get to a point where you have mastery over your credit—if you are in a position where you will have to utilize credit.

You must know how negative information and a positive payment history will affect your credit from day one, as well as how you utilize your credit, the time length of your accounts in your credit file and type of credit affects your credit and credit score.

Finally, you want to know how inquiries or the lack thereof, affects your credit and credit score.

By knowing what you must do comprehensively to make your dreams come true—you are showing that you are on path to doing what you need to do.

In life, nothing meaningful and significant comes easy! Therefore, you must decide at this time whether you are willing to put in the effort that is necessary to achieve at a higher level and bring the dreams that you desire into reality.

173)

Your ability to aim high and seek **goals that you may have never contemplated**—but you now decide to contemplate with a deep level of thought—may be what lights a fire inside your mind and heart and leads you on a more serious journey toward achieving what you desire while you are now on planet earth.

You must realize that you have untapped talents and abilities that are lying dormant in you at this time and are awaiting to be tapped into by you—**NOW!**

174)

You must realize that you too can use your thoughts and action to achieve the outcomes that you desire if you make

the decision to do so and you follow through on that decision in a <u>sincere manner!</u>

Climb higher, <u>reach higher</u> and <u>stretch your mind</u> toward what is truly possible as you <u>journey on planet earth</u>–the place of your birth and the place where **YOU** determine your self-worth–and the <u>net worth</u> that you desire, because **you control the decision** to reach higher and higher!

175)

You must use your mind to win in your financial life or any other area of your life that needs addressing <u>without making excuses</u> or providing reasons for your lack of success!

Whether you know it or not it is <u>your responsibility</u> to <u>transform your mindset</u> and <u>take the necessary actions that are needed</u> to ensure a prosperous and productive future for you and your family!

176)

Whether you are in sales or want to improve your life in a number of areas, you can use the following acronym to attain the success that you desire—just as I have used it over the past 20 plus years to attain success **(win)** on a consistent basis!

IDA B. WELLS

I—nterest—create interest in your product or service by taking initiative and having a superior product or service

D—esire—create desire by having a product or service that is needed by others

A—ction—create the need for others to take the desired action that you want them to take

B—elieve—you must always believe in your product or service and you must always believe in yourself

W—inning—you must always have a winning spirit—success must always be on your radar

E—nthusiasm—you must believe in your product or service and it must be a superior product or service if you are to present that product or service in an energetic manner

L—eads—by having a winning spirit and being enthusiastic about your product or service you will move in the <u>direction where success lives</u>—which will lead to lifelong success. In addition, you must have a highly effective system of getting sales "leads" that will take you to where you desire to be—and beyond

L—ife-long success—by doing all of the above you put yourself on a positive path to achieve your life purpose or achieve any other goal or objective that you may have in mind

S—uccess—by properly utilizing and understanding this acronym—success can truly be in your and your family's future

177)

In the case of reaching your goals or life purpose you must have Interest, or you must really want to achieve your goals— or life purpose. You must have a strong Desire to reach your goals or life purpose and you must take Action on a consistent basis so that you will reach your goals or life purpose—while you are here on planet earth!

And just as in sales—you must Believe in yourself, and you must believe that you will accomplish your goals or achieve your life purpose.

*You must also have a **W**inning and **E**nthusiastic spirit that will **L**ead you towards **L**ife-long **S**uccess!*

178)

"Winning" Is All About Making Good Decisions

It is important that you understand that sales (whether purchasing a product or service or selling a product or service) and life success (achieving any goal that you desire) is all about making decisions that are good for you and your family.

It is important that those who you approach with your product or service have a true "need" for your product or service. Otherwise, you will find yourself receiving bad publicity about your product or service.

179)

If you provide a superior product or service or you do something exceptional, that can often lead to positive publicity about your product or service!

However, you must not only have a superior product or service—you must fully believe in that product or service for your enthusiasm to come out when you present that product or service to others for their benefit!

The same is true as far as reaching your goals!

You must pursue goals that are meaningful and significant "to you" and "you" must believe that you will attain those goal(s)—in order to gain the "mental energy" that is needed to get your <u>focus</u> and <u>commitment level</u> where it needs to be!

180)

You must <u>pursue excellence!</u>

By pursuing your goals in a **more excellent way** you can put yourself in position to achieve lasting goals and give back or contribute to your favorite causes.

In a world that seems to be take–take-take you can become a giver. However, you must do the <u>"in between" or the "behind the scenes"</u> work **at your highest level of excellence** if you desire to achieve more throughout your lifetime and operate at a **higher level of excellence** on a more consistent basis.

181)

You must do a <u>detailed analysis</u> of your "<u>mental thought process</u>" and then make the decision to improve in areas that you are weak or deficient in.

You must do a sincere and honest self-analysis within "your mind" and you must realize up-front that it will take <u>constant effort</u> on your part to <u>cultivate the habits</u> that are needed for success.

You must have <u>self-confidence</u> and <u>self-discipline</u> at all times and you must let the enthusiasm or excitement that you now have on the inside of you—grow in an ever-increasing manner!

182)

By doing **a <u>detailed analysis</u> of your "mental thought process"** in a <u>sincere manner</u> you can put yourself in position for a **<u>winning future</u>** where you are in control and the success that you desire is the ultimate outcome.

Now is the time that you seize the opportunity to make great things happen in your life.

Stop for a moment and focus on what you want to achieve throughout your life, determine what you would like to do to help yourself, your family, and others— and make a serious commitment to start on a path to making it happen in real time!

183)

In some cases, you may have to let go to grow!

You must always realize that what separates the best from the rest is their daily thoughts and actions and whether they **make the choice** to operate daily at their highest level of excellence.

Isn't it time that you operate at your highest level in a way that makes sense!

You too have that same ability to choose–and act!

You no longer must lose–or be a hack!

Starting today you can choose to move forward in a better way!

Starting today you can choose excellence and get momentum to stay!

You and your family should have it no other way!

Excellence—it's inside of you!

Excellence, it's what you must pursue!

184)

It is important that you have the mindset that you want to consistently manage your credit and debt wisely and a **high level of commitment** is critical if you desire to **build wealth** more efficiently.

It is also important that you have a number of tips, insights and strategies that you can use consistently throughout your lifetime and you must recognize your **thought patterns** and understand fully <u>how you approach reaching</u> YOUR GOALS.

Your hollering, screaming, griping and otherwise negative actions on a daily basis does not change the fact that you are at this time where you are!

Don't let the daily criticism of others stop you from achieving what you truly desire!

Your daily exposure to the right information is what will really leave an impression on your mind and get you started on a path to **making the commitment** that you need so that you can achieve at the level that you desire.

185)

You must learn at each step of the way and continue with new ideas. Don't let your fears, the way you feel, your perceived lack of confidence, your desire to keep everybody happy or any other factor stop you from reaching higher and achieving what you desire at your highest level.

Your goal is to find the right information that you need to succeed—if you are now at a point in your life where you are ready to **commit to the success that you desire** at your highest level.

186)

By pursuing success at your highest level you won't worry about what others say or think about you as you will be

pursuing your goals at such a high level (you are doing what you direct your mind and heart to do at such a high level that you will be totally secure in the outcome) and you know deep within that you are **creating new opportunities** for yourself and your family.

The satisfaction that you desire can then be attained and **you will know** the success that you are pursuing depends on taking the right steps—consistently.

You don't have to do like others who have the attitude that "you can get all you can" and "can" all you get—and then sit on the can! You don't have to use force, gimmicks, or twist arms to get others to agree with you—or use other deceptive tactics to achieve what you desire because you know the steps that you must take to reach higher.

187)

If you <u>give it your best effort</u> you will receive what is best for you—however, you must also realize that the opposite is also true. *Isn't it time you make a dramatic change in your life!*

While pursuing your goals with a **high level of commitment** you must have the right attitude within your own mind, and you must have the right attitude with all whom you come into contact with as well.

Make sure you are committed to putting forth the required effort, otherwise you might as well remain on the sidelines!

188)

<u>Excellence in all you do</u> begins by you gaining the **<u>right habits</u>** and going the extra mile! You want to get to a point where you do more than is expected even when others don't. By doing so **<u>you will reach your goals more efficiently.</u>**

Make the decision to improve your habits in areas that you are weak in, and you can run the bad habits out of your life.

 Make the decision to **build wealth** in an intelligent, consistent, and proactive manner and you can achieve what you desire in a more efficient and effective way!

189)

Create and focus on big goals as the bigger your goal—the bigger it will be in your mind and the more effective guidance it will provide for your heart and mind!

Discipline and self-control are required of you and it plays a major role in determining if you are **truly committed** towards achieving what you really desire.

Say YES to your future! Say NO to now!

Your daily learning will show you how!

190)

You must realize deep within that it is **your responsibility** to take the **right actions** daily. It is your responsibility to find out what those right actions are. It is your responsibility to show and display the **discipline** and **focus** that is needed on a daily basis. It is your responsibility to **take action without delay** and reverse or eliminate the habits that you have that are **taking you the wrong way.**

You must realize that success rarely happens accidentally—it normally takes a concerted effort on your part—and it all starts inside of YOUR heart!

Are you **committed** on this day to take the right actions so that life begins to go your way?

191)

You must at this time make it a priority to know and understand your current credit and finance position so that you can purchase your home from a position of strength. By doing so you open up new ways and possibilities to manage your finances in more advantageous ways.

In order to know where you can possibly go you must first determine your cash flow!

By creating personal finance statements you can get a handle on your finances and make your home ownership period a much more enjoyable experience for you and your family.

192)

When you purchase your home you must know the true cost of ownership and that includes knowing the principal, interest, taxes, insurance, HOA, MIP/PMI, maintenance and all other associated costs.

You cannot purchase your home and underestimate housing costs such as utilities, water, electric, gas,, cable, garbage, storm water fees etcetera, as that underestimation can make your period of home ownership less enjoyable and more stressful for you and your family.

193)

The purchase of your home must be understood at a conceptual level and you must know what will or is most likely to happen from start to finish.

You must know your credit position, area of home purchase, environmental concerns within the home that you are considering for purchase along with environmental concerns in the surrounding area in which the home is located.

In a nutshell, that means you must know what to expect from prior to your loan approval to post closing!

By gaining this critical understanding proactively you put yourself in position to control the home buying process or any transaction in which credit is involved, as opposed to letting the process or transaction control you!

194)

It is important that you plan your home purchase with the end in mind, meaning you know prior to purchase how you intend to dispose of (or keep) your property (as best you can as life can be unpredictable).

You must know how your housing costs interact with the other areas of your finances such as insurance, investments, taxes, education planning, estate planning/wills, emergency fund and retirement planning so that you can achieve more during your lifetime.

By doing so you will be displaying a real commitment to determine your own future outcomes and success will be more likely to occur **throughout** your lifetime because you will have planned in a wise manner.

195)

It is important that you go into your home purchase in a sober manner and with the <u>clarity and vision</u> that you need to put yourself and your family in the best position possible to succeed.

By having a real understanding of the **pitfalls that you need to avoid** to make your home purchase a more successful one, you put yourself in the driver's seat <u>as opposed to being driven</u> in directions that are not of your choosing.

By <u>taking the right action at the right time</u> you can position yourself and your family for a more successful home purchase in this economy--or any economy.

196)

It is important that you don't become **complacent** and comfortable where you are now at.

The best time to gain the knowledge that you need is BEFORE you have to make a decision or choice, therefore it is imperative that you have a **proactive mindset** when it comes to managing your finances--and now is the time that you gain the preparation and knowledge that you need to succeed.

How you perform **when things are not going your way** will determine if you are a winner! If you are inspired and you decide to take the right action on a consistent basis, you can make positive change happen in your life.

Now is the time that you create and maintain success on a consistent basis and do what needs to be done on the front end!

197)

Be sure to let the empowering content that can be of benefit to you penetrate your heart and mind—so that you can more effectively apply what you are learning daily.

To achieve the success that you desire you must truly change your <u>thought pattern</u> and by doing so that can lead you to the success that will serve your and your family's best interests— not others who have no real connection to your and your family's life!

198)

Adversity will occur in your life that you never planned for, however you can overcome from the adversity that you will face (or that you are now facing) by

not being complacent and taking an active role in <u>ensuring that success</u> will occur in your and your family's future.

Are you operating in balance? Do your thoughts, feelings, behavior, and goals all line up with your values and beliefs? Are you moving towards the goals that will serve your best interest in an efficient manner?

By showing what you do with your time, your mind, your heart, and your management of your finances <u>you are demonstrating your sincerity and level of commitment</u> **toward reaching your future goals!**

199)

Is <u>your plan</u> for managing your finances <u>in sync</u> with your <u>thoughts and action</u> that you are taking at this time?

If what you are hearing, seeing and doing is <u>out of balance with where you truly want to go in your future</u>—you make the process of achieving your objectives much more difficult than it has to be—along with how difficult it should be!

Are you complacent in your daily activities? If you are, now is the time to change that!

200)

Are you <u>operating at a high level </u>on a daily basis and truly working towards your goals with a **consistent plan of action** that will take you to where you need to be? Do you know how to go over or around roadblocks to success or avoid them altogether?

By formulating a mental plan of action and then following up with a written plan you can **improve your focus** and get started on a path to truly **reaching your goals** in all areas of your life.

You must get to a point where you will do what you plan on doing in an **intelligent, consistent and proactive manner** or another way of looking at it is, you must use your mind at your highest level and get to a point where you will do what needs to be done when it is the best time to do so!

201)

When it matters most you must be in position to apply the knowledge and preparation that you have acquired to achieve the goals and outcomes that you desire in the most effective and efficient manner possible!

When you have a **consistent plan of action** that you utilize on a daily basis it may appear that you are going nowhere! However, in actuality you are going somewhere. And if you plan in an **intelligent and proactive manner** you can reach your goals much more effectively and efficiently.

You can then move in the direction of your life purpose or what you were truly put on earth to do. By taking the right steps on a daily basis you can do something big for yourself, your family and society.

202)

Today is the day that you make the decision or choice to take **<u>decisive action</u>** and not be **<u>complacent or content</u>** with where you are now at. Even if you feel you are very successful at this time, the ability to do much more resides inside of you.

Now <u>is the time</u> that you do what you need to do as you make a <u>serious effort</u> toward making your dreams come true!

203)

If you are considering starting on a financial planning journey with <u>written goals and objectives</u> and you don't have a history of utilizing **self-discipline** on a consistent basis—now may not be the best time for you to start on your financial planning journey if your goal is to achieve success at a very high level.

Be sure that you have mastered the self-discipline that is needed to achieve at a high level by having at least a recent history of doing what you say you will do on a consistent basis.

204)

If you are in an unfortunate position where you have poor credit, there are a number of relatively painless ways that you can enhance your **credit and credit score.** I say relatively **because it will take some effort and initiative** on your part to improve your **credit file and credit score** to a satisfactory level.

There are ways that you can legally remove inaccurate, negative and outdated information in your **credit file** and **improve your credit score and your ability to utilize credit** and get a better or the best rate when you engage in credit transactions.

For starters you can go to **AnnualCreditReport.com** and get a free copy of your **credit report from the three major credit bureaus.**

In addition you can find VALUABLE credit resources on the world wide web that can ease the burden of your credit management and help you manage your credit more wisely!

If you are sincere in your efforts and you are willing to take a little time out of your busy schedule, you can do much of what you need to do to **improve your credit and credit score yourself.**

In today's economy, credit influences many of our activities and you must know how to manage and **improve your credit file and credit score** effectively due to the importance that it will play in reaching many of your future goals.

Your credit score **(FICO Score)** determines if lenders will extend you credit and at what amount! The higher your credit score—the better off you are as far as utilizing credit as your fees on various types of loans will be much lower than those who have a lower credit score.

Building **solid credit** and properly establishing an **emergency fund** is at the foundation of transforming your life and operating daily in an **intelligent, consistent, and proactive manner.**

205)

Depending on the type of loan(s) that you have or desire to obtain—you could lose anywhere from hundreds to potentially thousands of dollars on an annual basis due to **poor credit and finance management.** Whether auto, credit cards, employment, home, insurance, rental property, utilities, cable, phone, or any other creditor— your ability to get a good or the best rate will be influenced by **your credit habits.**

*Some companies (including utility companies) will even **deny you credit** or require that you pay by debit card (or a monthly recurring debit from your* *checking account)* **if your credit is not at an acceptable level.**

Do your best to manage your credit in a proactive manner and be sure to avoid running up debt to an insurmountable level if at all possible.

206)

Thousands upon thousands of **credit grantors** such as credit card companies, retail stores, utility companies, apartment complexes and other lending agencies inform , Transunion, Equifax and Experian of their update activity on a monthly basis or when a consumer becomes delinquent.

The information sent to the **credit agencies** are your **credit usage patterns** including your payment history.   In the case of utility companies, apartment complexes and taxing agencies— negative information may be reported to TransUnion. Equifax and Experian if you become delinquent in your payment history, however your positive payments to them would not generally be included in your file.

Use this knowledge to manage your credit effectively throughout your life.

207)

If you feel that information in your **credit file** is **inaccurate, outdated, or unverifiable** you can dispute that information online or by mail. Be sure to include your personal information, name, address, social security number and date of birth and if mailing send it by certified mail with return receipt for legal proof that you mailed your dispute letters to the **credit agencies.**

By doing so you preserve the 30-day timeline which the credit bureaus must abide to by law! The credit bureaus must respond to you within the 30 days by law.

Be as clear and precise as possible by stating clearly what you are disputing and why! If you have added proof in the form of documents, cancelled checks, payment receipts etcetera—include a copy (be sure to keep the original) along with the **dispute letter** and be sure to keep a copy of the **dispute letter** for your records.

If you are now managing your credit effectively, continue to do so.

208)

After you receive the first collection notice, by law you have 30 days to request what is called "debt validation" and demand that the collection company prove that you owe the debt.

If there is **collection debt** in your **credit file** and it is **determined to be legitimate** by the **credit bureau** and you agree that it is legitimate and within the **statute of limitations in your state** you can possibly settle for a fraction of the amount and **improve your credit score and credit file some**—however, the approach for doing so is beyond the scope of this discussion.

209)

You want to positively affect your **credit file,** therefore be sure not to use your credit if your goal is to **improve your credit score** in a **timelier** manner. In addition, be sure to keep older accounts open as the longer the **Time** period a file with a positive payment history remains in your **credit file** the higher your potential **credit score.**

Be sure to stop using credit if your Cash Flow and Financial Position allows you to do so or use sparingly (quarterly or so) if you have a zero-balance card so that you can keep the account open, active, and part of your credit mix—so that you can improve or at a minimum maintain your credit!

210)

You want to have more than just one **Type** of credit (1 credit card and 1 installment loan is better than 2 credit cards) if you want to **build your credit score** at a faster pace. An auto loan for 2 years will be sufficient or an installment loan for other purposes for one or two years would be sufficient—just make sure the lender reports your activity to the **three major credit bureaus.**

- **Get a secured or retail credit card**

If you can't get a regular credit card or a retail store credit card (revolving loan) get a secured card and keep the balance low and pay off the balance as soon as you receive the bill! **Depending on your future goals and current credit position you may need to open several secured or unsecured credit card accounts!**

211)

After you remove negative and inaccurate information from your **credit file,** and you have at least 3 types (ideally) of credit open—you want to pay in a timely manner over a period of time. That time period will vary based on your **unique credit file.**

Be sure to **<u>get your credit file several times a year</u>** to see the progress that you are making and determine if you need to make additional moves in order to get your **credit score** at a level that allows you to reach your and your family's future goals. Only apply for **new credit** if it is a part of **your credit building strategy** or reaching your future goals as <u>too many **Inquiries**</u> based on you seeking new credit can lower your **credit score** some.

212)

It is important that you address your credit report comprehensively and you are disciplined along the way—as you must remain focused on your intended outcome.

It is also important that you realize that your credit file and credit score **is often used for insurance and employment purposes.**

With what you have just learned you have put yourself well ahead of consumers who manage their credit daily.

However, it is not what you have just learned that is important, but how you apply in your life what you have just learned!

213)

You must be aware of **credit repair scams** as they are prevalent throughout the **credit industry.** Be sure to visit the Federal Trade Commission prior to putting together your **credit restoration or credit improvement plan.**

The **Consumer Finance Protection Bureau** may also be able to assist you after you have disputed information in your credit file and the credit bureaus or creditor's do not respond appropriately after you have contacted them.

By doing so you can avoid many of the mistakes that unsuspecting consumers have made over the years and **find a template for creating and sending in dispute letters** that can help remove negative information that is inaccurate from your **credit file.**

After doing so you can truly be in position to manage your **credit scores, credit files** and your finances in an intelligent, consistent, and proactive manner and produce the outcomes that are in your and your family's best interest!

214)

It is important that you maximize your **discretionary income** monthly if you desire to achieve at a higher level.

By doing so you can put together a plan that will take you towards your future goals in a more effective and efficient manner.

If you have **discretionary income** (monthly income that is left over after the payment of your taxes and living expenses) at the right level you can save more for your future—whether it be increasing your emergency fund, saving for retirement or taking the types of vacations that you desire on a consistent basis.

You must not do like many who overspend (budget poorly) on a monthly basis and **do not have enough discretionary income left over** that allows them to do what they like to do or do what they NEED to do!

215)

If you plan in an intelligent and proactive manner on the front end you will know that your **"discretionary income"** is a key to your future success.

You can then put yourself in position to reach the goals that you desire in a more beneficial and reassuring manner.

You won't have the mindset of what might occur in your future as you can have certainty of your future outcomes if you know that you have the monthly income that you need to live at the level that you desire.

Do you at this time desire to get started on a serious path to success?

You can now do so—by choosing to give
it your best!

216)

*You can sincerely make it all happen by
<u>analyzing your monthly income and
expenses</u> and see where you are now at
as far as your discretionary income is
concerned.*

*Once you know you can devise a plan to
get more income, cut your expenses or do
a combination of the two.*

If your **discretionary income** is at the
appropriate level that allows you to live
your life in a manner that you are
comfortable at and still reach your future
goals you would know that you are in an
ideal position and the key to your
success would be coming up with a

workable plan for your future success and sticking to it on a consistent basis.

Understanding the **various forms of income** is critical for your future success and **understanding how to best utilize your discretionary income on a monthly and annual basis** where it will benefit you and your family the most, is critical for your long-term success.

You now possess in your mind a way to live your life more abundantly and it all starts with understanding the **various forms of income, determining your discretionary income on a monthly basis** and then deciding to do something significant and meaningful by saving more to meet your future goals—whatever they may be.

If you need more income, you may need to cut expenses or get more income to reach your goals.

217)

If your goal is to live the life that you desire you must realize at this time that **putting in motion** what you want to occur in your future is the starting point for you achieving the **excellence that you deserve** in all areas of your life.

If you make up your mind at this time to pursue your goals with zeal and you make up your mind to never give up, you will always defeat the negative forces that may come from the outside. Positive works on a consistent basis will always defeat negative energy that comes from the outside.

Your negative actions will achieve nothing meaningful, however your positive actions can push you in the right direction—even though they may not be totally consistent over time. If you give it your absolute best, you can still achieve what you desire in a timely manner!

You must decide now if you want a **"financial mindset of resiliency"** so that you can take off toward your destiny.

Always realize that adversity will occur in your life and be prepared proactively to still do your best in spite of the adversity that you will undoubtedly face.

218)

Many won't approach wealth building in a serious manner that will get them real results.

It is imperative that you approach wealth building appropriately or in a manner that can truly transform your future by **engaging your mind** at your highest level.

You must determine at this time to engage your mind at a higher level on a consistent basis!

Whether you fall into the category that does not engage their mind appropriately or the category that does, it is important that you gear your mind up for continuous success in your future.

219)

It is important that you realize that <u>how you look at your future</u> determines your access to the future success that you desire. Now is the time to stop, yield and do the right thing—consistently?

If your goal is to live the life that you desire you must realize at this time that **putting in motion** what you want to occur in your future is the starting point for you achieving the **excellence that you deserve** in all areas of your life.

220)

Do you have a mindset of resilience?

It is important that you realize that how you look at your future determines your access to the future success that you desire. Now is the time to stop, yield and do the right thing—consistently?

If your goal is to live the life that you desire you must realize at this time that

putting in motion what you want to occur in your future is the starting point for you achieving the **excellence that you deserve** in all areas of your life.

If you make up your mind at this time to pursue your goals with zeal and to never give up, you will always defeat the negative forces that may come from the outside.

Positive works on a consistent basis will always defeat negative energy that comes from the outside.

Your negative actions will achieve nothing meaningful, however your positive actions can push you in the right direction—even though they may not be totally consistent over time.

If you give it your absolute best, you can still achieve what you desire in a timely manner!

221)

Even if you are new to personal finance you want to find wealth building articles that are engaging and entertaining, but more importantly gets you the results that you desire or the results that you need to achieve to make your life more meaningful.

Your ability to simplify what many in the personal finance industry make complex and confusing could lead to you achieving more in less time.

You want to be particularly passionate about making the right choice on the front end!

By learning how to use the proper tools you can gain the knowledge that you need on the front end so that you can approach the management of your finances in a more intelligent, consistent, and proactive manner, thereby achieving your goals more often.

222)

If you are **passionate about your future** you will **Broaden Your Horizon** inside of your mind and have the **desire to achieve more** in your life! You can broaden your horizon and achieve much more right now by improving in the following areas:

- Inside Your Mind

Add value to others and it will provide opportunity for you.

You must obtain a system within your mind that allows you do what needs to be done daily in a more efficient manner—broaden your options and look at new and creative ways of achieving your goals.

223)

Perspiration—broaden your skills—hours —effort—study—practice—pay for above average material when it is in your best interest to do so.

- Inspiration

Discover what your true purpose for living is and create something new based on your own inspiration and pursue the direction in your life that is uniquely yours.

224)

Even if you feel unnoticed at this time in your life, it is important that you consistently give your best effort (you must **passionately pursue** what you desire in your life) as by doing so you are properly preparing your mind and heart for future success—all the while proving to yourself that you will be ready when major success occurs.

It is important that you don't sit by idly during your "waiting period" in your life during the "time period" where you are not where you want or need to be.

Patience is required; however, you must also do more daily to improve and develop your skills and grow daily.

225)

*Don't get frustrated by **adversity that will undoubtedly come your way** as it should be expected when you are trying to do something big!*

It is important that you walk in excellence on a daily basis and give it your best at all times as you act on the inspiration that you receive—when it is in your best interest to do so!

You must realize that if you give it your best right where you are now at—**your passion will come through** and your **"gifts"** will come to the surface and possibly be noticed by others at the right time and the right place.

226)

You must realize that "hidden greatness" resides inside all of us—waiting to be discovered by those who seek to find it—and pursue it!

You already possess many of the tools that are needed for major success <u>inside your mind</u> and you can develop the strength that is needed to achieve even more while you are waiting and discovering your true purpose.

It is important that you set goals in a **passionate and timely manner** if you desire to achieve at a higher level of success than those who fail to do so.

<u>**Time limits**</u> help create urgency within your mind and will help you achieve more.

227)

You must have courage as you move forward toward your destiny and putting a **time limit for completion** will give you **the courage that you need** to actively do what needs to be done in a more efficient manner!

You must have **"passion"** if you desire to achieve your financial goals and you must start right now and give it your best in all that you do!

Now is the time that you experience a "brain explosion" where you really look inside your mind and heart to **determine in a sincere way** what you desire in your future so that you can create more certainty in your future!

You must have **the passion on the inside of you**—if you really want to make your dreams come true.

You have the ability, capability, and capacity to do much more during your lifetime, however do you have the audacity to **passionately go after your dreams** at this time?

228)

It will be a great contribution to humanity when you **sincerely decide to pursue your hidden greatness** and find your true gift that you need to share with the world!

You must have the mindset that you will do your best and **passionately pursue your goals**—even on days when you don't feel like giving it your best.

By passionately pursuing your goals you can make the right things occur in your life!

It is important that you realize that the vast majority don't achieve their goals because they don't really know what they want—therefore, **even when they have passion**—it is misdirected and won't lead them toward their true purpose.

You can avoid that mishap by determining what you really want out of life and pursuing what you really want out of life at this time **in a passionate manner!**

It is important that you know where you are at in your **"life stage"** and know the moves that you can make to enhance your future and position yourself and your family properly so that you can enjoy life more abundantly and do what you were put on earth to do.

229)

It is important that you consistently grow, mature, flourish and find your purpose in your life. You don't have to let others determine your future.

You don't have to live in uncertainty and confusion about your future by not knowing if you will reach your goals— both financial and otherwise!

You must have a resolute, secure, and stable view of your future and you must have an **unwavering passion** to put in place and pursue—what needs to be pursued at a level that is the best that is within YOU!

Isn't it time you embrace something bigger than yourself and pursue it in a **passionate manner?**

230)

It is important that you have **a plan of action** to make your future goals happen and **you must put that plan into action in a passionate manner.**

Passion must come from inside of you and there must be something big that you want to see come true. Passion and desire must come from inside of your heart; therefore, you won't be afraid to start!

You must not *wait on getting the OK from others!*

If you desire to improve your finances in an intelligent, consistent, and proactive manner--you must leave all excuses behind!

It is also important that you realize that **what you desire or really want to occur in your future** can't be taught—**it has to be inside of your heart!**

231)

Now is the time that you **pursue what you really desire** on a daily basis so that you can **passionately** reach your life purpose and achieve at a much higher level.

You will soon be amazed at the success that you will achieve based on a **small step** that you decide to take at this time. By **passionately pursuing your goals in**

your life you can turn something small into something big.

Your challenge is to pursue your life purpose and financial goals with a high level of passion on a daily basis—so that your future is enjoyable in the right places!

232)

You must always realize that who you once were and who you are now **are not synonymous**—and who you will become will be determined by you and **how passionately you pursue what you desire in your future**—whether it be financial or otherwise!

It is imperative that you pursue what you desire with passion and fire—and always have the presence of mind to reach higher!

233)

It is important that you realize that the "steps that you take" to improve your finances can lead to what you feel is initial success—but **ultimate success** never occurs!

Your goal is to attain **ultimate success** in your **wealth building efforts** and achieve at the higher end of your potential.

Your **ultimate success** in your **wealth building** efforts require that you look at and act on your finances in a number of critical areas that is your responsibility to know!

234)

You must know <u>your monthly inflow and outflow as it relates to your finances</u> and by knowing what you take in and pay out on a weekly and monthly basis you set yourself up for success and you put yourself in a better position to achieve the **ultimate success** that you desire to occur during your lifetime!

You must create a personal budget, income statement, balance sheet and statement of net worth and use the result of that analysis to manage your finances more effectively based on a <u>written plan of action</u> that will lead to your future satisfaction!

If your income exceeds your expenses on a monthly basis you are in position to <u>pay off debt</u>, <u>save for your future</u> or do

[215]

other creative things as it relates to your finances that will take you closer to the **ultimate wealth building success** that you desire.

If your expenses exceed your income on a monthly basis, you must cut expenses, discover ways to come up with more income and/or do a combination of the two.

You must do all of the above using the most accurate financial data as possible-- if you sincerely desire to make your dreams come true.

235)

You must have an effective understanding of the 5 credit factors and you must know at all times that you must keep **negative information** off of your credit file, keep your **utilization or your use of credit** at a low and manageable level, know how the **"time factor" affects your credit,** know the **types of credit that you have and why that is important** and know **why you must keep inquiries to a minimum** if you are in the process of building your credit.

You must not lackadaisically manage your credit. You must be an active participant in the management of your credit and by **mastering the 5 credit factors** mentioned above--you put yourself in real position to do just that!

236)

You must know that if you "know about" and manage your insurance, investments, taxes, education funding, estate planning/wills and retirement planning effectively throughout your lifetime you can achieve much more.

You must also understand the importance of creating a properly funded emergency fund so that you can put yourself in position to achieve major success throughout your lifetime!

By having a comprehensive understanding, you can soar and improve your financial and wealth building score!

237)

You must have an awareness of how you are utilizing your mind or mental approach as you manage your finances and build wealth. You must realize that you can do much more on a daily basis once you gain a **"comprehensive awareness"** of your finances and "you" determine that you are willing to expend more effort to manage your finances.

You can increase your <u>mental energy</u> in a major way by <u>shifting your mindset toward what is really important</u> in making what you desire to happen--occur! You don't have to achieve the type of success that is fleeting--or a little more than a blur (short-term success)!

238)

Your effective understanding and pursuit of attaining true success as it relates to managing your finances more effectively and building your wealth more efficiently is contingent upon you making a concerted effort to <u>understand in clear terms</u> what it takes to attain **ultimate success**—as you build wealth.

You cannot leave your **wealth building future** to chance and now is the time that you take a strong stance!

You cannot do like others who wander through life in a manner where they see their finances clearly in one area or certain areas, but do not have a **comprehensive overview** of their finances that allows them to see their future with the view that they need--and deserve!

You can now start on a path to attaining the **ultimate wealth building success** that you need and deserve—without having to navigate a sharp curve!

239)

It is important that you utilize your mind in a manner that is of high intensity and is focused on the success that you desire. Your daily focus must be so strong that the success that you desire is the only "possible" outcome!

You must ask yourself what can I use to help reach my goals more efficiently and effectively and how can I achieve <u>winning success</u> in all areas of my finances?

You must imagine yourself being unstoppable in your pursuit toward the wealth building success that you desire—and using your mind to look at your finances from a fresh new perspective that is not the norm could be what is needed in your life that can turn your current situation into that of greater success.

240)

By asking and answering the **"right questions"** you can help bring what you visualize and sincerely want in your and your family's future—into reality!

You want to analyze what you can do now to work toward building wealth in a responsible and rewarding manner where your and your family's success is at the forefront!

It is important that you draw up in your mind a **realistic outlook** of how you will get to where you want to go as you journey toward **building your wealth** more intelligently.

241)

You no longer must ask — "Can I" manage my finances and achieve the Wealth that I need and desire—the question soon will be, will I manage my finances more effectively now that I possess the knowledge that is needed to do just that?

Asking and answering the right questions stimulates your thought process and provides your mind with new insight on accomplishing your future goals.

You want to determine what you can do **right now** to work toward achieving your future goals and **building wealth** in a more efficient manner.

242)

Listen to the inspiration within and act on it when it is in your best interest to do so.

The process of how to get through adversity and how to conquer what ails you is your responsibility!

Are you in need of re-focusing your thought process so that you can achieve more?

The empowering and enhancing qualities that are needed by you to achieve major success already resides inside of you. You must strive to always attain righteousness—not only when it becomes acceptable to others, but always!

243)

Even those who currently have a **high net worth** could achieve far more if only they had an effective system in place that allowed them to manage their monthly income and expenses in a more intelligent, consistent, smarter and more beneficial manner.

By creating a **realistic plan for success,** you will know your monthly income and your monthly expenses and you will have an understanding **within your mind** of how to manage your income and expenses effectively so that you can reach your desired goals.

By knowing your income and expenses monthly, you can put a plan in place that will allow you to reach your future goals in a realistic way and not just base your future goals on wishful thinking or improper planning.

244)

By utilizing a monthly cash flow statement (budget) you can pursue your future goals with more focus and commitment and **build wealth** in a more effective manner because you will know your "financial numbers" and you will be in a better position to see your future more clearly and reach your desired goals.

Setting meaningful and significant goals and creating a pathway to reaching those goals that are realistic and based on your own unique monthly income and expenses are critical for you and your family **if you are sincere** in really reaching your goals.

Keep in mind that due to life events or other factors that you may not have control over—you may have to modify your goals and/or the timetable for reaching them. However, you must not be discouraged, and you must continue to move toward the goals that you desire to attain.

245)

You must balance your goals and at the same time use wisdom in your approach.

It is important that you look at your finances in a comprehensive manner— even while creating your budget and establishing your emergency fund as it will help immensely in your goal setting efforts.

Insurance Planning, Investment Planning, Tax Planning, Emergency Fund, Education Planning, Estate Planning/Wills and Retirement Planning will all come into clearer focus once you create a monthly budget and you know the amount of your discretionary income!

246)

You must realize that the more diverse your investment mix—the more the odds are that your plan will stand the test of time. Consider index funds as well as actively managed funds, CD's, I-bonds and other bonds and money market accounts and be sure that you are comfortable and have a real understanding of how what you are investing in works.

Be sure to use tax-advantaged accounts and tax advantaged contributions to your maximum benefit!

And above all decide right now—and know within your mind and heart that **the time to seriously approach your finances and achieve your dreams**—will NEVER be just right!

247)

By deciding to take control of your **Wealth Building** future **right now**—you can put yourself in position to control your future and **increase your returns** and do what you really want to do during your lifetime—and at the same time you minimize letting others control your future and enhancing their bottom line at your expense.

Now is the time that you use your creativity (ideas, insight, <u>inspiration</u>, concepts, <u>dreams</u> etcetera) to move forward and get your future right.

*By **building your wealth** in a more thoughtful and intelligent manner you can achieve much more in your future!*

248)

You now possess ideas and insight within your mind and heart that puts you within reach of making your and your family's future a much more prosperous one.

*You can now do far more to work toward **building your and your family's wealth***

*and achieve much more during your
lifetime.*

Always remember that if you desire to
build your wealth more effectively you
must have a system (within your mind)
that allows you to create a personal
budget, create a personal income
statement and create a personal balance
sheet and you must know your personal
net worth at this time—so that you can
get MOMENTUM rolling—if you are to
achieve at your highest levels.

249)

You must use the information that is
derived from your personal finance
statements as a major tool to help you
formulate **written goals** that can make a
real and lasting difference in your life
and lead you and your family forward in

building wealth in a more efficient manner than if you had not done so.

You must make up your mind at this time to really pursue (take the right action on a daily basis) what you desire in your future with all of your might and every fiber in your body!

Now is the time that you dig deep and stretch your mind and heart further than you've ever stretched before—**by doing so the success that you always dreamed of will be just behind the door!**

250)

You can achieve major success, and that success will be due in large part to the **decision that you made** to open your mind up to what was possible and looking at your future in a more engaging and prosperous manner so that you could **build your wealth** in a more intelligent, consistent, and proactive manner.

251)

You must realize that if you <u>aim low</u>—those are the results that will show!

If you <u>aim high</u>—you can exceed the sky!

If you make a <u>real commitment</u> to do your best—you can <u>achieve a high level of success!</u>

If you make the <u>decision</u> to <u>do less</u>—your life will likely be a mess!

Use the <u>abilities that you have inside of you</u>—to make your <u>credit and financial dreams</u> come true!

252)

*You don't have to approach your
financial future with
a <u>cluttered</u> or <u>fearful</u> mind or approach
your future in a manner where you lack
understanding—<u>unless you choose too!</u>*

Did you know that effectively managing
your finances helps you manage your
stress—or negative energy and improve
your quality of life significantly?

You must realize that **thousands across
the globe have already utilized sound
management of their finances to change
their future to that of true success and
you can do the same**—if it is your desire
to do so!

253)

There are many who need help in the management of their credit and finances and those that pursue success in a sincere manner can learn how to do so in a very efficient and effective manner!

Your focus is on the consistent and constant improvement of your finances so that you and your family can benefit in an even more effective manner and in a manner that will lead to even greater success for you and your family.

254)

Rarely will you find an approach to wealth building that is uniquely designed for **your success in today's economy** and an approach that is designed to **get you** the results that **you desire** in the most cost-effective, time-efficient and easy-to-follow manner possible!

If you find that approach you can take your future in the <u>direction of success</u> that can lead to real and lasting success for you and your family!

255)

You have the "ability within" <u>**to analyze**</u> <u>**your credit and finances in a more**</u> <u>**critical and accurate manner**</u> **and**

therefore put yourself in position to attain the success that you need or desire to attain!

You can **put your mind in position** to **know** what **you need to do** on a consistent basis so that you can gain the financial freedom that you know you deserve.

256)

You can expand your credit and finance knowledge and gain the preparation that you need to succeed throughout your lifetime.

You now have the opportunity to expand your thoughts and you can put yourself in position to effectively understand personal financial statements— effectively understand how credit works—and effectively understand <u>all of the areas of your finances that you must address</u>—if you are to attain major success in the management and improvement of your credit and finances.

257)

Why let worry, fear and anxiety dominate your thoughts on a daily basis when you have the ability to change that and <u>dominate your thoughts </u>with <u>success</u>, <u>faith</u> and <u>certainty</u> as it relates to your credit and financial future--and life?

You can manage your credit and finances in a comprehensive yet efficient manner and improve your financial position in a manner that serves you and your family the most—not creditors and others who could care less about your existence other than the payments that you make to them!

258)

You could use your mind more effectively!

Now is the time that you take back your mind and use it to make great things happen in your and your family's life!

Even if you are now facing adversity, you must not **use that as a reason or excuse** to not take the "right action" that can lead to you enjoying life on your terms!

You must realize that the adversity that you are now facing or that you may face in your future will make you stronger in the long run—if you believe it to be so!

259)

Do you have a <u>"financially alert mind"</u> or are you slow to act when it comes to managing your credit and finances?

You must realize that it is <u>your responsibility</u> to use your mind in a manner that benefits you and your family the most—not creditors and others who have no real concern for your or your family's future!

260)

Do you know that you have the ability to control your mental focus and attitude and enhance your future for the better?

Did you know that when you know you can succeed you don't worry about failing or what others may think?

The knowledge of how to attain the success that you desire can be found on the inside of you. It is up to you to discover it and work toward making your dreams come true. You can <u>choose to</u> over-use your mind, use your mind appropriately or under-use your mind.

261)

Your over-use of your mind (not literally as you can never truly do so) will provide you the opportunity to achieve what you desire.

Your under-use of your mind will hold you back and you will join in the long line of <u>those who complain daily</u> because they are unwilling to utilize their mind and take daily actions to see what they really could be—and attain what they truly deserve!

Did you know that you can use your mind, direct action and mental focus to attract what you desire on a daily basis? What are the "abilities" that you now have or are determined to get?

262)

Did you know that if you change your thoughts and daily actions you can change the direction of your credit and financial future—right now?

It is important that you look for and expect success on a daily basis! Did you know that daily griping and grumbling will only lead to your stumbling?

Now is the time that you start addressing the issues of concern in your life so that you can avoid financial strife.

263)

Now is the time that you move forward—toward your reward and improve your scorecard!

Did you know that if you are breathing you have the opportunity to change your future right now?

If you are now in need of improving your credit and finances you now have the opportunity to do just that.

By taking action you have the opportunity to manage and improve your credit and finances to a higher level on a daily basis!

264)

Now is the time that you give it your best! Now is the time that you put your mind to the test!

Always remember that success is not for you if you are not for success!

You must transform the world and after you do so it will be too late for others to affect the outcome. Now is the time that you determine if success is for you!

265)

You can now get your financial future going right.

You can do so at your convenience and at your pace without added pressure or cost other than your valuable time if you find the right approach!

You will achieve success by doing what you need to do on a consistent basis.

266)

You will soon discover that **you can** do much more in your life daily.

Are you letting what has been passed down from others set limits on your life—or are you using what has been passed down as a base point for you to grow and <u>create an atmosphere for greater opportunities and results</u> in your life?

By analyzing <u>how you manage your cash flow on a monthly and yearly basis and taking inventory of what you now own</u>

and what you now owe to others, you can determine future moves that you can take to help stabilize and improve your financial position.

267)

The key point that you must realize is that to attain the success that will lead to the achievement that you desire is all about getting "it" right on the front end—not after you make mistakes!

The "it" is whatever you feel is important in your and your family's life whether it be financial or otherwise.

268)

Success as it relates to your "credit and finances" consists of knowing your responsibilities and acting on that knowledge to improve your credit and finances in the most efficient and effective manner possible!

By mentally comprehending and acting on the knowledge that will serve you and your family in an advantageous way— you put yourself in position to attain the success that you desire--today!

269)

Improving your credit and finances to a high-level means that you have mastered what it takes to move yourself and your family forward in an efficient and effective manner.

In some cases, you may have to let go in order to grow!

You must always realize that what separates the best from the rest is their daily thoughts and actions and whether they **make the choice** to operate daily at their highest level of excellence.

Isn't it time that you operate at your highest level in a way that makes sense!

You too have that same ability to choose—and act!

You no longer must lose—or be a hack!

Starting today you can choose to move forward in a better way!

Starting today you can choose excellence and get momentum to stay!

You and your family should have it no other way!

Excellence–it's inside of you!

Excellence—use it to make your dreams come true!

270)

- Do you understand the need to create personal financial statements **and use them for your and your family's greater benefit?**

- Do you have a "mental system" of managing and improving your credit that is highly effective **and a system that you can utilize at your convenience?**

- Do you have a mental system that allows you to know all areas of your finances **that you must address at this time—and in a comprehensive manner?**

Answer the above questions appropriately and you are well on your way toward ultimate success!

 271)

By having a clear <u>credit and financial focus</u> you put yourself in position to attain the success that you desire—regardless of your definition of success.

You will be in position to see your credit and financial future in clear terms and in a way that provides you the <u>clarity</u> that you need to succeed—in today's economy!

272)

By having a clear <u>credit and financial focus</u> you will be in control, and you will be able to **achieve success** at a level that you desire and by default that level is at a higher level than you are currently at! You can **achieve success** at a high level if you <u>prepare your mind for the journey</u> and you gain the right knowledge that leads to you taking the <u>right action</u> towards the <u>goals and objectives</u> that are most important to you and your family!

273)

Success can now come your way!

Will you get started today?

You can now **achieve at a high level** and reach the success that you desire for yourself and your family if you make the decision to really **seek goals that are meaningful** and can move you and your family forward at this time!

274)

Do you have the skills that are needed to manage and improve your credit and finances in today's economy?

Understanding your credit and finances in today's economy is vastly different from what it was just 10 years ago!

You need a system and approach that gives you the ability to manage and improve your credit and finances in the times that we now live in!

Do you have a system and approach that allows you to do just that?

275)

Your goal is to find unbiased credit and financial advice and approaches that have worked for consumers from around the world!

You want to learn how to save and invest properly, how to improve your credit, how to purchase and sell your home properly, and how to build your net worth to a high level—among other concerns!

The ability to save properly, improve your credit, purchase, and sell your home properly, and build your net worth can be found by your diligent search and your willingness to use your mind to achieve more.

276)

The missing ingredient in your financial management is the decision by you to take your achievement to the highest level that you can by using your mind and heart to take <u>direct action</u> on a consistent basis—and really apply what you need to apply!

Your goal is to obtain the <u>proper preparation</u> and <u>knowledge</u> that is needed and <u>increase your determination</u> to understand and apply that knowledge so that you can achieve more—in a more comprehensive manner!

277)

You can now gain an understanding of how cultivating <u>the habits of success</u> can lead to **"achieving"** your goals in a more efficient and effective manner!

Do you know that if you show <u>"sincerity"</u> <u>in your efforts</u> to apply what you are learning in a <u>determined manner</u> on a consistent basis—major success lies in your and your family's future?

*<u>Now is the time</u> that you make the decision to achieve the **<u>credit and financial goals</u>** that will serve your and your family's best long-term interests!*

278)

By approaching your financial management with excellence as the goal, you are not leaving your finances to chance, but you are moving toward your goals in a more excellent way because you are systematically approaching your finances and you have a definite timetable for achieving your goals that are measurable.

By pursuing your goals in a **more excellent way** you can put yourself in position to achieve lasting goals and give back or contribute to your favorite causes.

In a world that seems to be take–take-take, you can become a giver.

You can achieve <u>untold success</u> in your future and you can **achieve** just that by applying what you are learning in an <u>effective manner!</u>

279)

It is important that you <u>leave the stress behind</u>, and take inventory of where you are now at. You must be prepared to give it your absolute best to improve your situation as best you can.

It is also the time to look forward and find other ways manage your finances more effectively and you must realize that financial planning should be a year-round activity for those who desire to achieve more.

Start strong, cultivate habits of success, move forward—maturity is knowing when to stop foolish behavior.

280)

You must look forward toward success and settle for nothing less!

You must now give it your best go so that the results that you desire will show!

You must really go after your <u>credit and financial goals</u> *this round—and not be deterred by obstacles or roadblocks that slow others down.*

You now have <u>or you soon will have all that it takes inside of you</u> to navigate your way forward and make your dreams come true!

Success is now on the way because you have <u>made the decision</u> to <u>want more</u> today!

281)

You must at this time live your life daily knowing with certainty that any **obstacle** that comes your way will not affect your plans—or cause a major delay—in any way!

<u>Now</u> is the time that you do what you need to do and now is the time that you <u>learn something new</u>!

By doing so, you can equip your mind properly and **overcome any obstacle** that you are facing or that you may face—and <u>make your dreams occur at a faster pace</u>!

282)

If you believe success lives in you—
success will believe in you. You must feel
worthy of all the **success that is in your
future.**

When <u>proper preparation,</u> <u>know-how,</u>
<u>execution</u> and <u>faith</u> meet inside of your
mind and heart—"success" will say—
<u>WELCOME!</u>

283)

Always remember that you have the
"power" to take your mind to a <u>"good
place"</u>—you don't have to stay in a <u>"low
place"</u>—if you <u>make the choice </u>not too.

**In short, you are worthy of whatever
you decide in your mind, that you are
worthy of!**

284)

Always remember that many can quote wise thoughts, very few can <u>apply wise thoughts effectively</u> and in a manner that can transform their life.

You can <u>aim high or aim low</u>—no one else can control your aim—you control how you feel about yourself and the <u>direction</u> that your life will take!

Use that knowledge to control your future <u>and stop blaming others</u> or let how others look at you and feel about you affect your life in a detrimental way!

Use that knowledge to free your mind from anything in your past or your family's past that may be holding you back from reaching your goals!

You have the <u>mental capacity</u> to do great things in your life—you don't have to live your life in strife!

285)

Greatness is In You (Give it Your All)

No one can see what you see or do what you do.

You are a unique creation—the world is waiting on you!

Your gifts and talents can be seen all around.

Please don't let us down!

We want to ensure that your gifts are around.

Will you do (be) all that you can—and not let us down!

Your gifts and talents are our reward.

For you not to give it your all, would not lead us forward.

Use your creativity and not negativity—you'll receive a positive charge—and go down in history—as large.

Is it any wonder that you have what it takes?

You can be all that you want to be if you don't put on the brakes!

Do you know that you are great?

Provide us your gift (purpose) for being here—the world can no longer wait!

Do you know that you have the strength that you need—to succeed?

Greatness is in you—you can make all your dreams come true!

Starting today—will you do what you need to do?

286)

You must realize that hope, wishful thinking or prayer—without action is not a strategy and you must know that major success can be in your and your family's future by taking appropriate action and doing what you need to do—on a consistent basis!

Putting a plan in action that is measurable and has definite deadlines

for achievement is a strategy—if done properly!

287)

You can <u>demonstrate faith</u> and the fact that you value your and your family's future by <u>taking action at a high level</u> and <u>achieving at a high level</u>—right now!

You and your family are **worthy** of a prosperous and successful future—now is the time that you <u>affirm that reality!</u>

288)

By <u>having faith that you can achieve your goals</u> you can change your life and the <u>direction</u> that you are going—right now!

The key to your success is not the knowledge that you will gain—but how

you **"comprehend" and "utilize the knowledge"** that you will gain in your daily life.

While learning something new—it is important that you engage your heart and mind at your highest level, and you use your willpower to take the appropriate action that you need to take on a consistent basis.

289)

Use your imagination and say to yourself—why not me—you should be saying why not me—if there is something big in your future that you really want to see become a reality!

You must realize that you can't wait on others to tell you that it is OK to create what you desire in your future!

290)

By being original—<u>thoughts at a high level </u>will be in your midst on a consistent basis and if you <u>act on those thoughts</u> in a meaningful way, you can take your life in the direction of your life purpose.

291)

It is important that you act on <u>inspiration</u> that comes from within when it is in your best interest to do so. And you must feel that you are **worthy** of the success that you desire, regardless of the area that you decide to excel in.

292)

Do you know that you are worthy of whatever you think you are worthy of?

Do you know your purpose for your life at this time?

Answer the right questions appropriately—and use the knowledge that <u>you will learn daily</u> to reach your highest heights as you move towards the success that you desire for yourself and your family!

293)

You must be <u>diligent in your approach</u> as well as <u>vigilant in your approach</u> and <u>you must be fully committed</u> to achieving your goals at this time!

You can excel—you can come up and out of any situation that you are in if you have the <u>proper mindset!</u> You must be excellent in spirit and always move forward—**mediocre goals must not be a part of your mindset.**

294)

If you diligently work toward your goals and you do not let <u>distractions negatively affect you</u>—you will gradually improve and success will occur if you are consistent in your approach towards working toward your goal(s)!

295)

Pursuing excellence (winning) requires <u>focus of thought</u> and the <u>decision by you</u> to operate in <u>excellence</u>! It is the intentional use of your mind to enhance the probability of the outcome that you desire.

296)

You must have positive thoughts, <u>you must believe in yourself at a very high level</u>, you must get back up and make the best of your situation—<u>NOW!</u>

You must excel, you must move forward, you must focus daily, you must get better—you must pay attention to the details!

You must **plan for your success!**

297)

Whether you know it or not it is <u>your responsibility</u> to <u>transform your mindset</u> and <u>take the necessary actions that are needed</u> to ensure a prosperous and productive future for you and your family!

It is important that you have a certain level of knowledge as you pursue your <u>wealth building</u> efforts. Although you don't have to be an expert, you must have a yearning or strong desire to achieve optimally as it relates to building wealth.

You can increase your **K**nowledge level, **E**nthusiasm level and obtain the **G**uidance that you desire, so that you can truly reach higher and avoid a financial fire!

298)

You must <u>pursue excellence!</u> You must not only possess the knowledge that you will gain in your mind, but you must also comprehend and use that knowledge on a constant basis if you are to attain true success!

You must do a detailed analysis of your "mental thought process" and then make the decision to improve in areas that you are weak or deficient in.

You must do a sincere and honest self-analysis within "your mind" and you must realize up-front that it will take constant effort on your part to cultivate the habits that are needed for success.

299)

You must have self-confidence and self-discipline at all times and you must let the enthusiasm or excitement that you now have on the inside of you grow in an ever-increasing manner!

By doing so in a sincere manner you can put yourself in position for a **winning future** where you are in control and the success that you desire is the ultimate outcome.

300)

You must know what you need to always do when it comes to managing and improving your credit and finances and, in this MILLENNIUM, —it is more important than ever that you get it right on the front end.

You must make it a priority to gain the "mental working knowledge" that is needed on a daily basis to attain <u>success</u> at a high level.

By doing so you will know how to avoid bad decisions that consumers make on a constant basis without even realizing they are making a bad decision!

301)

You must understand that if you gain the **proper preparation** and the **proper knowledge** on the front end, you gain the insight that is **essential for success** in today's economy!

*You don't have to let **anxiety and uncertainty** rule your life and by preparing properly you can avoid financial strife!*

By increasing your knowledge base about your finances in an intelligent, consistent and proactive manner, you are preparing your mind and heart for a more successful financial management future where the skills that you gain can be applied effectively.

302)

You need to know that <u>Disposable Income</u> **differs** from <u>Discretionary Income.</u>

It is very important that you **distinguish in your mind** that disposable income is money that you have left after paying your taxes—while discretionary income is money you have left over after paying your taxes "and" mortgage/rent, food, utilities, and life's other necessities.

Discretionary Income is money that you can spend or save at your discretion!

303)

Did you know that you can increase your income by **making compound interest work for you** and not against you?

By understanding and being able to distinguish among the various types of income and understanding how compounding works—you put yourself in position to understand your personal finances in a more meaningful and effective manner!

You also put yourself in position to control your future in a more "financially alert manner" and in a manner that will lead to true success for you and your family!

304)

Always remember, that a high level of **dedication** will lead to a high level of results when you are pursuing your credit, finance or any other goal or objective that you may have!

You achieve more when you set goals—limitless and largely untapped areas of accomplishment can occur—if you remove limitations from your mind and you set meaningful goals!

305)

You must understand that it is difficult to do what needs to be done on a daily, weekly, and monthly basis to improve your finances to a high level. However, by <u>applying the right knowledge</u> you can gain the <u>mental fortitude</u> that you need—to succeed!

You must bring a strong desire and willingness to not only learn what you need to know; you must also be willing in a strong way to <u>apply what you are learning</u> when it is in your best interest to do so–thereby providing you the potential to truly grow.

You must at this time gear your mind up to pursue your goals with passion, as by doing so you can open a new door and achieve so much more!

You must turn up your motor and rev up your motivational level so that you can put yourself in greater position for success.

306)

You must get to a point where you can set a goal—no matter how small—and actually pursue and achieve that goal.

That will then give you the confidence that you need and if you continue to set and reach your goals consistently, you will develop the **habit of self-discipline** that is required in your financial and other areas of your life.

You will then have the real belief that you can achieve your <u>**retirement goals,**</u> <u>**pay off your debt in a timely manner,**</u> <u>**save for your children's education**</u> **in an efficient manner or reach any other** <u>**goal**</u> <u>**or objective**</u> **that you may have for yourself and your family.**

307)

You must pursue <u>your credit and</u> <u>financial goals</u> with the real expectation that the goals that you seek in your credit and financial life will <u>"really occur"</u> in your life!

You must pursue your credit and financial goals with real passion, you must really want to <u>achieve the goals that you set</u> deep down in your heart (your intellect, will and emotions must really be involved at a high level) after you have given <u>serious thought</u> to the goals that you want to achieve!

When you are operating in a sincere manner <u>you can more effectively direct your future!</u>

308)

When you are operating with "true sincerity" towards your credit and financial goals you can <u>see the vision</u> (your goals) occurring and you can feel it happening.

You have no doubt that what you are seeking will really occur because you are <u>pursuing your goals</u> at such a high level and you have the <u>preparation</u> and <u>knowledge</u> that is necessary that success is the only outcome that is possible!

You cannot deceive yourself; you must pursue your goals with a very high belief that the goals that you seek—will occur.

309)

It is important that you use **any adversity** that you may face as an "energy force" to dig deep down into your spirit to see how you can do things in a better and more effective way!

Do not do like many and get down for a prolonged period and get a feeling of hopelessness when **adversity** occurs!

If you understand how **adversity** works you would realize that on many occasions that **when adversity occurs** it is the time to challenge your mind to reach higher heights!

310)

Once you understand that when adversity occurs it is the time to challenge your mind to reach higher heights—you must <u>take actual steps</u> to reach higher heights in your own life.

You must realize that when **adversity** occurs there is also an opposite end of the spectrum that lies in the horizon that could mean great success and benefit for you and your family—if you believe it to be so.

However, <u>if you lack the motivation to take action</u> and you do not have the **"<u>vision</u>"** to see that the **adversity** that you are facing now—normally has a benefit of "equal or greater value" in your future—you may not **respond to adversity** in a manner that benefits you and your family the most.

311)

You must remember that "every" adverse situation that you face also creates an opportunity—if you believe it to be so!

It is important that you understand that those who respond favorably to **adversity** on a consistent basis will set themselves up for untold success in the future if they look at **adversity** from the vantage point of adversity working for their benefit—not against it.

312)

If you want to be in the successful group that responds favorably to **adversity** on a consistent basis you must always remember in your heart and mind that **adversity** <u>makes you stronger</u> in the long run—not weaker—although you may feel weaker for a certain period of time.

Be sure that you use any adversity that comes your way as fuel to move yourself and your family forward!

313)

In the most difficult of adverse situations, it can often be difficult to believe that there is a greater benefit ahead for you, however—if you do, success is in your financial future.

If you have the proper mindset, focus, and understanding of how the economic system in your country works **and you know how to properly respond to adversity** you can improve your credit and finances to a high level.

314)

Starting today never look at an **adverse situation** as one that is to your or your family's detriment.

Quite the contrary—you must look at the **adversity** that you are now facing or that you will face in your future as an opportunity to reach higher heights in your life—whether it be in your personal finances or other areas of your life!

You must pursue your path to success with more precision and following a path

<u>that is proven</u> and will get you the desired results and take you where you want—or need to be will go a long way in helping you reach your goal(s).

315)

If you are facing an **adverse situation** now, it is important that you <u>do not let your current situation stop you from reaching your and your family's future goals.</u>

Whether you are or are not facing **adversity** at this time you can improve your credit and finances to a high level!

You can get to where you and your family need or want to be <u>in an efficient manner</u> if you are <u>truly sincere</u> about improving your and your family's credit and finance position.

316)

You must know that when you face **adversity**—a vision is often born or developed—if you look at **adversity** as a time to look within and do something meaningful and significant and not get down on yourself?

Keep in mind that when you decide to do something meaningful in response to the **adversity** that you have faced in your past—or that you will face in your future—it may take time for that vision to materialize—as real success normally occurs over time.

Therefore you must stay focused and realize that the vision that you see—**will occur!**

317)

We have seen many who faced **adversity** go on to do great things—with new and empowering visions that they <u>put into action</u> that positively affected the lives of many.

Even though the vision that you may have after facing **adversity** can't save everyone—it can provide what is needed to help those who respond positively to your vision and those who see—**what you see!**

Your vision can make a real difference in the lives of many and can help those that receive your vision attain a higher level of success!

318)

By positively responding to adversity and <u>creating a powerful vision</u> you can get the minds of many <u>moving in the right direction</u> and get their mind in the right mental environment—where "<u>success</u>" lives.

You must realize that as a result of facing great adversity and then <u>making the decision to respond to that adversity in a powerful and forceful manner you can discover hidden talents and abilities and achieve goals that you never thought possible!</u>

319)

You must have "real insight" on how you can do great things in your life if you "respond to adversity" in the appropriate manner!

Now is the time that you **overcome any adversity** that you are facing and go on and do great things—so that you can transform your and your family's future to that of real success on a consistent basis from this day forward!

320)

You must have the attitude that you will use your "mental energy" to search out and find the best system available to improve your credit and finances—whether a cost is involved—or not!

You must be intelligent in your thoughts and think as accurately and analytically as possible!

You must know, believe, and have faith that success is the only possible outcome in your life if you really believe that success lies ahead for you and your family.

321)

It is important that you realize that there are many who are in need of transforming their finances and gaining a better understanding of how to more effectively manage and improve their credit and finances.

However, there are only a select few who actually want to <u>change the direction</u> that they are going and actually start on a path to significantly improving their credit and finances.

It is your <u>responsibility</u> to bring the proper focus, commitment level, motivational level–<u>and other successful qualities to the table</u> if you desire to <u>achieve at a higher level</u> and sincerely reach the goals that you desire most.

322)

Very few will follow through with the <u>determination</u> and <u>commitment</u> that is necessary to change their situation in a meaningful and significant way to benefit themselves and their family for generations.

There are many who know what to do and still fail to do what needs to be done—or what needs to be done on a consistent basis!

Are you among the few?

323)

Do you have the <u>self-control</u> that is needed for success?

Are you willing to change the way that you approach and manage your finances?

What if you were to discover that there is <u>a more excellent way</u> to do so at this time?

A key component to your future success is knowing what to do and when—and knowing what not to do—and when!

324)

Are you willing to make small adjustments daily in order to pursue something big in your future?

Do you have the perseverance—determination and other qualities that are needed so that you will stand strong during times of adversity or when difficult times come—or are you going to quit?

Are you **willing to make every effort** and are you doing all that you can to reach your and your family's <u>written goals and objectives</u>—or are you just kidding yourself?

325)

What do you see in your and your family's future?   Do you have real faith that you will <u>attain what you see?</u>

Do you have the perseverance, <u>preparation</u> and <u>knowledge </u>that are needed at this time—or are you in need

of further cultivation of those <u>and other qualities</u> in order to reach your and your family's goals?

You can't share the right knowledge with others if you don't have the right preparation and knowledge yourself!

326)

You must realize and know that you were created to succeed and you can attain goals of real significance right now <u>if you are highly motivated</u> to do so!

You can put yourself in position to help others, reach your retirement goals, pay off your outstanding debt and attain many other goals that you may feel are out of reach if you decide now to get the preparation and knowledge that you need to succeed on the front end and not after you make costly mistakes!

327)

You have the gift to bless others and you can grow in your knowledge of managing your finances in an effective and efficient manner—<u>if you choose to do so!</u>

You must do so in an energetic and enthusiastic fashion!

Are you growing and producing daily? Are you challenging your mind daily? Do you wake up excited or are you dragging your feet to even get out of bed?

Depending on your answer, you may need to learn a better approach if you sincerely desire to get ahead!

328)

Why look back and wonder if you did all that you could with the gifts and talents that you had?

You already know (or soon will know) that it takes discipline, sacrifice and a sincere determination to reach meaningful and significant goals.

It is important that you also realize that you may have to scale back or spend less time doing what you really like to do in order to achieve the goals that you desire!

329)

Do you have the desire in your personal life to achieve your life purpose and achieve at a high level at this time?

You must know that perfect timing is created by you—the time to do anything meaningful will never be just right—unless you make it just right in your mind even when things are not just right in actuality!

You must use the opportunity that you now have to change your situation and utilize your talents and abilities and if you dream big and set big goals—you put in motion what is needed to bring those dreams and goals into existence!

330)

Why wait on others to do what you have the ability within to do yourself?

You must do it yourself! You can do it yourself! However, you must take the first step to get the ball rolling.

You can achieve phenomenal success in your future if you put in the work! Are you making the sacrifices that are needed and are you doing what you need to do daily?

331)

Do you realize that if success was easy, we would all be successful? If we could attain success by thinking about it, praying about it, dreaming about it— etcetera, we would all be successful?

Do you realize that "true success" takes work—and taking the right action—on a consistent basis?

The time to choose success is now!

332)

Now is the time that you move to action! Your ideas, dreams, hopes, aspirations and what you really desire can occur!

Now is the time that you pursue your goals and achieve at a higher level. You can do it step by step and ultimately achieve the success that you desire!

You can turn an adverse situation into success if you embrace what you are now facing and gain strength from it. In the end you will find that the difficulty that you are now facing or that you may face in your future will be a part of your success story—if you believe it to be true!

You have the drive on the inside to move forward and you must harness your willpower and move forward!

Is your mind your biggest enemy? If you are not **moving to action** in the right manner consistently—it might be!

Now is the time that **you say yes to that big dream** that lies in your future! Now is the time that you turn potential into actuality and reality!

333)

Now is the time that you realize that you are worth <u>what you think you are</u>

worth—and now is the time that you reach for and attain the goals that you truly desire!

Now is the time that you **properly focus** on what you can do—not what you can't do!

Now is the time that you realize that you are receiving information and advice that can truly change your life—whether it be for your credit, finance, real estate or any other concerns.

334)

You need to learn a system or approach that can take you to where you need or desire to be <u>in an efficient manner?</u> From this point forward you no longer have to let <u>worry</u> and/or <u>fear</u> rule your <u>thought process</u> on a daily basis!

You must do your "due diligence" and do what is reasonable by critically analyzing your finances at this time and do what you feel will serve your and your family's best interest.

335)

You must ask yourself—what is out there that can be of the greatest benefit to you and your family in a highly beneficial and cost-effective way as it relates to credit, finance and real estate?

You must then choose among the best and then make the decision to utilize the knowledge and understanding that you will have gained to work toward achieving the success that you desire for yourself and your family!

You must make a way—find a way— discover a way and make your future goals a reality!

336)

You must make a way—find a way— discover a way and make your future goals a reality!

You must know the "mental process" that your mind must go through—if you are to achieve success at your highest level and you must have a willingness to go through that process within your own mind!

After putting into effect plans for improvement of your finances in all areas, it is important that you continuously review to more effectively ensure that your dreams will come true.

By looking at how you have <u>progressed or regressed</u> with your finances, <u>you can get your mind</u> to come up with new ways of looking at and solving <u>financial dilemma's</u> that will undoubtedly occur as you are in the process of building wealth.

337)

You can accomplish your goals in a more <u>efficient and effective manner</u> by knowing what you need to focus on and what you need to avoid.

You want to know the importance of **dreaming big** and pursuing your goals at your highest level as that is good for not only you—but your family—and future generations as well!

Your view of yourself and your situation is the starting point for you transforming your credit and financial future and improving your financial situation significantly.

338)

You must do what you are empowered to do—right now—to make your dreams come true!

The ability to take the right actions reside inside of you!

The ability that is now within you (or soon will be) is there to help (power, strength, enthusiasm) you achieve your goals.

However it won't happen without you taking action!

339)

You must do what you are **truly able to do** and you can then take your success to a higher and higher level!

It is important that you realize that success may not come in the way that you want—but it will often come in a different way than you desire or expect!

You must always realize that success or failure often depends on <u>how you handle or respond to adversity!</u>

340)

Success, true happiness, peace, and joy is internal! Failure is internal! Your mindset and how you view what you view determines whether success or failure is in your future!

You have the <u>mindset to achieve your goals and objectives!</u> You have the mindset to <u>see your future clearly!</u>

The <u>timing is now right</u> for you to achieve those goals and objectives that you really desire and those <u>goals and objectives</u> that can really be of benefit to you and your family!

341)

You have **no other alternative** if you **properly focus** and you gain the **preparation** and **knowledge** that you need—**to succeed!**

It is important that you realize that regardless of where you are now at—you can **re-focus your mind for success** or adjust your mind and daily habits to achieve more in your life. You possess the ability to achieve at a much higher level daily and it all starts with using your mind and heart in more engaging and creative ways!

342)

Ambition is a true quality that can help effectively propel you and your family towards your financial and life goals.

Many consumers lack **ambition** at a high level and by having a **lack of ambition** they make their and their family's financial journey more difficult.

By having a high level of **ambition** towards reaching your financial and life goals, you set in motion the inner workings of your mind and activate your mind and heart towards reaching the goals and objectives that you seek!

343)

With the **proper ambition** you will move toward your financial goals and objectives with the real expectation of attaining them.

It is important that you are ambitious and focused as you move toward achieving your and your family's financial and life goals.

A **high level of ambition** will lead you to pursue other positive and highly effective qualities in an effective manner.

344)

If you **lack ambition,** you are in effect making life more difficult for yourself and your family.

It takes a <u>high level of belief,</u> <u>know how</u> and <u>determination</u> to reach your and your family's financial goals!

Wisdom is the skillful use of knowledge and <u>knowing what to avoid and what to confront</u> is a great way to approach wealth building if you are one who desire to operate at "peak performance" as it relates to your wealth building efforts.

Why make mistakes yourself and prolong your journey to financial freedom when you can <u>learn from the mistakes of others</u> and achieve success more efficiently?

The real use of empowering information is in the <u>execution or acting</u>—not gaining the knowledge alone! Keep that understanding at the forefront of your thought process!

345)

A high level of ambition will help you reach your and your family's financial goals more effectively and more efficiently.

Ambition forces you to <u>move to action</u> and by doing so <u>you activate positive momentum</u> that can help you and your family <u>reach heights that you may have previously thought were unattainable.</u>

You must be <u>determined</u> to <u>put into action</u> what can really move you forward! It is imperative that **<u>you have a clear understanding of wealth building basics</u>** and how you can use the basics of wealth building to more effectively direct you toward your goals!

346)

By having a **high level of ambition** you are saying to the world— "I will attain my goals and objectives in an effective and efficient manner" and success will be in my future!

It is important that you don't let others negatively affect your **ambitious spirit.** You must remain focused and disciplined as you move toward your future success.

347)

It is important that you don't let others negatively affect your **ambitious spirit.** You must remain focused and disciplined as you move toward your future success.

By having a high level of ambition, you are making a strong statement to

yourself, your family, and others that you intend on making success a reality for yourself and your family.

Always make it a point to shape your future in the manner that is best for you and your family.

348)

By having a high level of ambition you can put yourself and your family in position to take that vacation at the time of your choosing and at the place of your choosing, <u>attain your retirement goals,</u> purchase that vacation home and provide assistance to causes that are important to you and your family.

A **high level of ambition** will give you the <u>energy that is necessary</u> to move you toward what is truly important in your and your family's life.

349)

Always remember that ambition and success is inside of you—if you believe it to be true!

Ambition is a quality that you should strive to attain and if you apply it at a high level, you can avoid financial pain!

Make it a point to achieve your goals today—you and your family should have it no other way!

350)

With a high level of **ambition**—you can put yourself and your family in the right financial position!

By developing **ambition** at a high degree—you will attain positive results that you can see!

Use the **ambition** that you have on the inside of you—to make your and your family's financial dreams come true!

You can achieve untold success on this day—you and your family should have it no other way!

351)

You must control your anger and use your mental abilities in the appropriate manner.

Controlling your anger **helps you manage your credit, financial and life stress more effectively—if you "control your anger" on a consistent basis!**

In life there will be times when <u>you will wonder</u> why the <u>wealth building success</u> that you desire to happen is not happening when you want it to.

Even so, <u>you must not complain</u> or be weary. By <u>reflecting back on the financial decisions that you have made in your past</u> you can set yourself up for a more prosperous future.

By reflecting on your past experiences, being more discerning on what you expose yourself to <u>"at this time"</u> and improving on your <u>"mental thought environment"</u> you can put yourself in position for a <u>more prosperous</u> future.

352)

Your anger about your situation does nothing to solve the deficit issue.

It is easy to be angry—however it takes **strength to reverse your anger** and control your mind to make real change and success happen in your life!

Living your life daily with **anger inside** of you does nothing to improve your (or your family's) credit and finances to a high level.

Quite the contrary—you **magnify the anger** inside your heart and mind and make reaching your goals more difficult!

353)

You can **reverse the anger** that you have inside if you don't let anger fester in your spirit. You can **reverse anger** by forgiveness, kindness and tenderness and your life will change for the better.

If you do a good deed to someone who hurt you, which is a hard assignment in many cases—you can start on a path of releasing and reversing the **anger** that you have inside of you.

Peace, joy and happiness can occur and remain in your life if you learn from your past and make a sincere effort to improve your future.

By reflecting back on your money management skills, how you manage your credit and how you manage your finances from a comprehensive perspective, you open up real possibilities for achieving real success, now and in your future and you can reverse anger for your and your family's greater benefit!

354)

**If you "truly and sincerely" want to
transform your credit and financial
future you must see yourself controlling
your anger and believing in your
heart that future credit and finance
improvement can and will really
happen!**

It is very important that you realize "right
now" that you can control your actions
now and achieve so much more as it
relates to your financial future and the
building of wealth.

By gaining control of your finances at the
earliest time possible, you can position
yourself to acquire more assets during
your working years, protect your assets,
and gift your assets while you are alive
and even after you transition.

355)

You must realize that it will take a high level of <u>discipline</u> to achieve the success that you desire!   However, the **anger** in your spirit will go away if you take the right action on a consistent basis.

Likewise, you must release and reverse your <u>poor money management skills</u> and get started on a path that will lead to lasting success. You will <u>reach your goals</u> in a timelier manner and that could help free up time so that you can <u>sincerely do</u> what you <u>enjoy</u> and live out your life in a <u>more bountiful</u> manner.

356)

You must believe in your heart that you can **control your anger** (if that negative quality applies to you) and improve your credit and finances to a high level.

You can get started now on improving your credit and finances and it is important that you have a long-term perspective of why you must manage your finances comprehensively, along with a plan of how you will manage your finances more efficiently.

You must also have a plan in place to periodically review—if you truly desire to make your dreams come true. By doing so you can leave worry, anxiety, fear, frustration, lack of effort and procrastination behind you—exactly where it should be.

357)

If you have **anger** festering in your spirit you can alleviate some of the **anger** by **reversing the anger** in the direction of joy—by forgiving others, treating those whom you come into contact with on a daily basis with kindness and having a spirit of success.

Real success will begin to happen in your life if you change your focus and you are determined to make real success happen for yourself and your family.

358)

You must realize that you must focus and pursue your goals at a high level on a consistent basis!

Are you <u>exceeding in what you are supposed to be doing in your life at this time</u> (your life purpose) or are you exceeding in **what you want to do?**

Always realize that time is one of the greatest gifts ever given to you—and you have the ability to **<u>control how you utilize your time</u>** as well as **<u>control your daily actions</u>** as it relates to effective management of your finances.

You must realize that you can **<u>do far more than you are currently doing</u>** when it comes to the effective management of your finances.

You control your <u>thought</u> process, the <u>decision</u> making as it relates to what you are <u>willing to learn</u> and the <u>actions that you will take</u> on a consistent basis.

*You control how you will **save and invest** and **address your finances** in a comprehensive manner!*

359)

As you move toward your financial goals you should not feel stressed out or frustrated about your finances and a proactive approach to managing your finances will help significantly in controlling how you feel on a daily basis.

There must be congruence and agreement within your mind and heart on "what you think," "what you say" and "what you do" if you <u>sincerely desire</u> to make your wealth building dreams come true.

If something doesn't feel right in your finances or you feel your finances are out of balance, you can correct that by analyzing your current situation and coming up with a serious plan that you believe in and you are committed to implementing in your life!

360)

Are you using your full potential that God has given you?

If you are willing to follow the crowd you will never be able to tap into your full potential.

Whether you move against the wind or have the wind at your back as you pursue your goals, you must equip your mind to make the right decisions—consistently.

Even a dead fish can flow downstream without any effort! However, upstream requires effort as you must take action to get to your destination.

In a like manner, we can all feel good and go with the flow when the rhythms of life are flowing in the way that we desire!

However, can we feel good when the currents are coming our way and still achieve what we desire?

You are awesome in an unrelenting way as you have completed the reading of these axioms to help direct you in a more effective way from day to day.

Go out and be all that you can be, you are now equipped to dream bigger than any star that you now see.

Reach higher, achieve what you desire, avoid a wealth building quagmire—and give it your absolute best from wire to wire (throughout your stay on planet earth)!

Publisher: TFA Financial Planning

Email: tj@TheWealthIncreaser.com

ISBN: 978-1-953994-18-9

APPENDIX A

Thomas (TJ) Underwood—Real Estate Broker, Financial Planner, Author, Blogger

Thomas (TJ) Underwood is a real estate broker, former fee-only financial planner and loan officer who has served consumers in the Atlanta metropolitan area and throughout the world.

He has created over 700 pages of web-based content, created several books and e-books, and continues to provide timely blog articles that have helped many around the world.

His inspiring, informative, entertaining, and highly beneficial articles have assisted visitors worldwide since 2010.

Thomas (TJ) Underwood blogs regularly at www.TheWealthIncreaser.com and offers real estate brokerage and financial planning services to paying clients at his Atlanta office.

If you are interested in having Thomas (TJ) Underwood prepare a debt payoff or comprehensive financial plan, please phone 404-952-9284 or email tj@TheWealthIncreaser.com to schedule an online consultation that will remain confidential.

You can also learn about other services that are offered by going to the following site:

https://www.thewealthincreaser.com/tfa-financial-planning/

If you desire to create a debt payoff or comprehensive financial plan yourself and would like a blueprint of how you can create your own, email tj@TheWealthIncreaser.com and put your debt payoff or comprehensive financial plan request in the subject box and he will respond to your request.

APPENDIX B

Thomas (TJ) Underwood/

TFA Financial Planning

Thomas (TJ) Underwood has created over 700 pages of credit, finance, and wealth building articles covering the entire spectrum of personal finance on three websites.

The three sites have brought forth a new version of financial planning that turn the odds in your favor (not creditors) and more importantly puts you in control of your finances and wealth building activity in a way that could lead to greater success for you and your family throughout your lifetime.

With 2010 being the year of "when the blogging career of Thomas (TJ)

Underwood all started" it would only be appropriate to provide **10** additional topics that could further lead to you achieving lasting success in the next ten years and beyond.

In the paragraphs below you will find **"10 success principles that came to mind as this book was being finalized"** that can help you achieve your financial (and life) goals at a higher level "in this and the coming decades" while you are here on planet earth.

- **Know what to avoid**

It is important that you manage your finances from a standpoint of understanding **what** you need to avoid.

You cannot let worry, anxiety, fear, frustration, and lack of effort dominate your mental space.

By purchasing this book and frequenting www.TheWealthIncreaser.com and other wealth building sites you are showing a real commitment for successful outcomes to happen in your future.

- **Know what to confront**

In a similar manner to knowing what you must avoid in order to achieve optimally—you must also know what you need to confront. You must prepare your mind for success by gaining the right knowledge and using that knowledge appropriately.

You must not only have that knowledge—you must actually confront

your current cash flow position, your credit understanding and your financial understanding in all areas—if you desire to achieve optimally throughout your lifetime.

- **Have a big imagination**

Nothing can hold you back more than your inability to dream big—and pursue those big dreams!

You must formulate significant goals and **have every intention within your mind** of achieving those goals.

- **Know your thought process**

How do you approach your finances and financial future? Do you even have an approach?

By **thinking about your future and what lies ahead** you put your heart and mind in position to receive the vibration and rhythms of life that can lead to "life happenings" going your way.

- **Begin with the end in mind**

You must begin with the end in mind whether it is a car purchase, home purchase, educational goals, retirement goals or any other goal.

By doing so you put yourself and your family in a more favorable position for success.

Will I sell or trade in my vehicle in 3 years?

Will I stay in my home for 20 years and then move to my dream location?

Will I begin saving now to help fund my child's educational needs 15 years from now?

Will I allocate my risk profile with my investments in an appropriate manner? Will I sell stock X that I bought at $5 per share—all or in part—when it hits $20 a share?

Will I choose mutual funds, or will I use a stock portfolio to help reach the goals that I desire—or will I use a combination of investment vehicles to reach the goals that I desire?

Will I save appropriately so that I can reach my "retirement number" so that I can do what I desire in my retirement years?

The above—and **other probing questions** based on the goals that you are pursuing are what you must ask on the front end—so that you won't suffer on the back end!

- **Always know the importance of your credit score**

A good score generally starts at around 700 and the higher you go after that point the better.

You get into the great or excellent range once you score 750 or higher and that would put you in position to get the best rate in most transactions that involve credit.

Your mastery of the 5 credit factors that you have learned in this book has positioned you for the success that you desire at the various stages of your life as it relates to your credit and credit score.

- **Keep your monthly bills under 10 so that you can win**

You must make it a point to manage your bills monthly (mortgage, auto loan, gas, electric, water, garbage, phone, cable, and credit cards) at an optimal or highly effective level.

Keep in mind that if you are at nine bills or twelve bills you are still ok—the goal is 10 or so per month—to add clarity to your mind and thought process so that you reduce stress on a daily, monthly, and annual basis.

You must have **clarity** and **focus** on a daily basis and not allow clutter to cloud your mind!

By keeping the number of bills that you pay from your checking account on a monthly basis **under 10**—you set your living circumstances up <u>so that you can win.</u>

This success principle does not mean that you can't have other accounts to reach your <u>ultimate goals</u> such as an account for entertainment and living outside of your "fixed monthly expenses" or investment accounts and other accounts that are designed to help you reach your goals.

- **Know your money management personality**

By knowing how you manage your finances on a daily, weekly, monthly, and yearly basis—you put yourself far ahead of those in the general population who go about their daily activities in a manner where they don't have a clue.

Are you a **highly effective money manager**—or do you need to improve?

There is no need to panic as you can achieve lasting success regardless of your money management style.

- **Know where you are at in your life stage**

Whether you are just entering the work force, just graduating from college—or you have been working for years—it is important that you understand **the stage in life** that you are at.

By doing so you add clarity to how you see your future and you make reaching many of your goals more likely to occur.

- **Always establish a properly funded emergency fund**

It is imperative that you **establish an emergency fund** at the earliest time possible, and properly fund that emergency fund.

By doing so you help reduce the future risks that you will face in your life and success will be more likely to occur.

- **Have faith that what you are pursuing will truly occur**

You must know and act consistently in a manner that says to the universe—I will succeed!

You must **sincerely pursue the goals that you desire** so that you can give your mind added incentive—to reach higher!

You must believe and know that the results that you are pursuing—will show!

It is important that you use your **experience, expertise and you exercise the use of your mind in a spirit of excellence** if you desire to achieve more during your lifetime.

And just as "that process" led to the creation of three leading financial blogs, numerous books and e-books—and increased profitability for Realty 1 Strategic Advisors and TFA Financial Planning—so too can you use that process to make big things happen in your life.

Even though the **year of 2010** (my first year of blogging) started on an upbeat note with the creation of www.the-best-atlanta-real-estate-advice.com and later that year www.realty-1-strategic-advisors.com, the author of **Wealth Building Axioms Volume 1** would face great adversity in the spring of 2010 when the mentor of the creator of **TheWealthIncreaser.com** transitioned and _even greater adversity_ later that same year when the younger brother who looks just like the author of **Wealth Building Axioms Volume 1** unexpectedly transitioned in the fall of 2010.

Those unfortunate events tested the faith of the author of **Wealth Building Axioms Volume 1,** however by responding positively to adversity in the same manner as I have urged you to do in this book—the continuous development of a number of sites took on a new meaning and increased urgency—and brought forth over 700 pages of web content that you can now benefit from at this time along with the creation of a number of books in "The Real Estate & Finance 360 Degrees Series of Books" that are now on the market.

Always realize that the success that you desire often begins by looking within and giving **serious thought** to what you desire most in your future. You must leave "all" excuses or reasons why you can't reach your destiny behind you, so that you can take the necessary steps toward making your dreams come true.

You must open your mind up to the inspiration (and always be open to receiving inspiration when it is in your best interest to do so) that will follow and you must have a strong desire on the inside of you—to make your dreams come true.

That initial thought at a deep level can lead you on a journey toward making the right moves <u>at the right time</u> and more effectively guide you toward your destiny!

In the end (or maybe the beginning depending on where you are now at) it is your timing, your willingness to move to action, your preparation, your focus, and an unstoppable belief on the inside of you—that will guide you in the direction of doing what you definitely need to do—to make your dreams come true.

Use what you were enshrined with at birth <u>(a spirit of excellence)</u> while you are here on planet earth!

It is of the opinion of the author of **Wealth Building Axioms Volume 1** that this book will act as a springboard to success and will help you achieve many of your financial goals.

However, you must realize that the opinion of the author of **Wealth Building Axioms Volume 1** is biased in favor of the author.

You must determine for yourself whether **Wealth Building Axioms Volume 1** is the best book for you—or whether there is another book on the market that will work better—as far as making your dreams come true.

Always remember that the burning desire that you have on the inside at this time (or at some time in your future) to do "something big" may be the voice of God giving you the "ignition" that you need to help direct your steps and give you added strength to bring something new and powerful into this world—at a time and in a manner that is uniquely designed for you!

All the best to your continued success in the next ten years in your life—and beyond...

APPENDIX C

Advanced Credit and Finance Strategies

To continue your quest to improve your financial position, you may want to acquire additional books and resources that are a part of the real estate and finance 360 degrees series of books. Here's how:

www.TheWealthIncreaser.com

Currently **The Real Estate & Finance 360 Degrees Series of Books©** *consist of:*

Book 1) Managing & Improving Your Credit & Finances for this Millennium Paperback **Copyright© 2012**

Book 2) HOME BUYER 411 *The Smart Guide to Buying Your Home*

E-book **Copyright© 2014, 2023** Hardback **Copyright© 2023**

Book 3) HOME SELLER 411 *The Smart Guide to Selling Your Home*

E-book **Copyright© 2014,2023,** Hardback **Copyright© 2023**

Book 4) The Wealth Increaser E-book **Copyright© 2014,** Hardback **Copyright© 2023**

Book 5) The 3 Step Structured Approach to Managing Your Credit & Finances E-book **Copyright© 2014, 2023** Hardback **Copyright© 2023**

Book 6) The FIZBO Manual (For Sale By Owner Guide) E-book **Copyright© 2014, 2023** Hardback **Copyright© 2023**

Book 7) 1-2-3 Credit & Me E-book **Copyright© 2021, 2023** Paperback **Copyright© 2023,** Hardback **Copyright© 2023**

Book 8) Credit & Finance Improvement Made Easy E-book **Copyright© 2014, 2023**

In addition, you can find helpful articles on several credit and finance topics by visiting the following websites:

www.the-best-atlanta-real-estate-advice.com

www.realty1sa.com

www.TheWealthIncreaser.com

I welcome your success stories and the positive effect that the books in the series along with the articles on the websites have had on your life.

Copyright© 2024

Publisher: TFA Financial Planning

Email: tj@TheWealthIncreaser.com

ISBN: 978-1-953994-18-9

Wealth Building Axioms Volume 1 will help you:

- **Utilize effective ways of thinking so that you can stay focused and build wealth in a more rewarding manner.**

- **Provide insight on how you can utilize credit and build wealth in a way that puts you in control and keeps you in control.**

- Change your life in a major way by providing you new ways of looking at credit and finance so you can achieve your goals in a way that will allow you to achieve major success in clear terms so that you will look at your finances from various angles so that you can get on a more serious path toward making your wealth building dreams come true.

Thomas (TJ) Underwood is the Real Estate Broker at Realty 1 Strategic Advisors LLC, one of the most successful real estate and financial planning companies in the metropolitan Atlanta area. Realty 1 Strategic Advisors is based in Peachtree City, Georgia.

He is a former fee-only financial planner and top producing loan processor, and he has assisted clients from as far away as Germany with their financial concerns. The axioms in **Wealth Building Axioms** *Volume 1* have been utilized by savvy consumers to enhance their credit understanding and achieve many of their major goals in a timelier manner.

He is also the creator of **TheWealthIncreaser.com**, one of the leading financial blog sites that can be found in the internet universe.